COLLINS LIVING HISTORY

The Making of the United Kingdom
1500-1750

Christopher Culpin
Series editor: Christopher Culpin

CollinsEducational
An imprint of HarperCollinsPublishers

Contents

UNIT 1	The new monarchy	page 6
UNIT 2	People and homes	18
UNIT 3	Kings and Parliaments	30
UNIT 4	Searching for a settlement	42
UNIT 5	Restoration London	54
	Glossary	62
	Index	63

attainment target

This symbol appears with questions which are targeted at the attainment target for history. At the end of Year 9 you will be given a level in history on the basis of how well you have answered these questions.

Some questions are about how much you know about different periods in the past: how people lived and what they believed. Others are about how things change through history and why these changes happen.

People are always trying to describe the past and sometimes they say different things. You will be asked about these differences and why they occur.

We find out about the past from historical sources. You will be asked about how we can use these sources to reach conclusions about the past.

Introduction

The picture below shows Lord Cobham, with his wife (on the left), his sister (on the right) and their six children. The painting was done in 1567, when the children were aged (from the left): two, one, six, twins of five, and four.

When Lord Cobham was born in 1527, Henry VIII was on the throne and England was a Roman Catholic country. As he grew up he saw England become Protestant, and many other changes. Lord Cobham died in 1596, but his children would have seen relations between kings and parliaments worsen in the 17th century. Their children would have lived to see England and Scotland united in 1707. These are just some of the events described in this book.

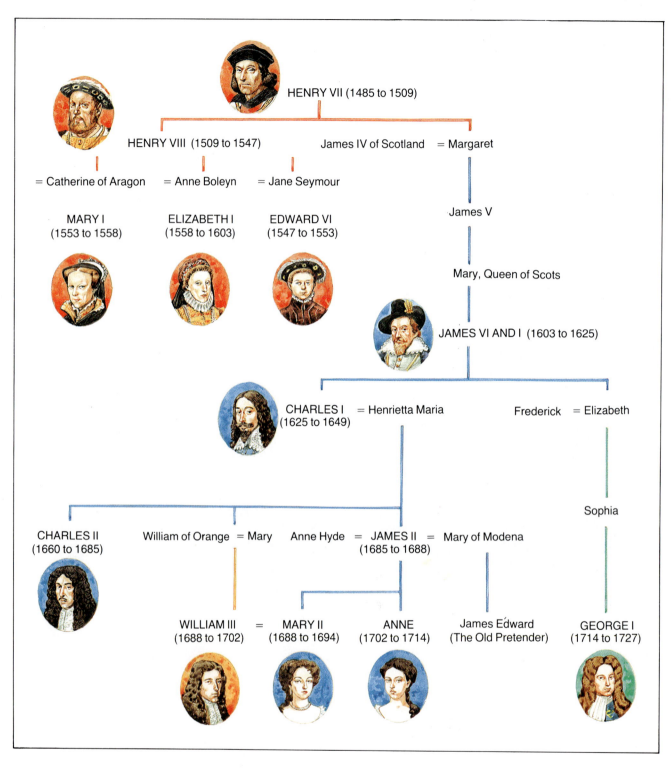

In the family tree of the Tudor and Stuart monarchs above, the Tudor family is shown in red and the Stuart family in blue. Those members who reigned as monarchs are shown in capital letters. The lengths of their reigns and some of the important events in them can be found in the timeline on page 5.

TIMELINE

1520 Field of the Cloth of Gold

1534 Act of Supremacy
1536 to 1540 Dissolution of the Monasteries
1536 to 1543 Acts of Union with Wales

1588 Bible translated into Welsh

1605 Gunpowder Plot

1620 Pilgrim Fathers go to America
1628 Petition of Right
1638 English Prayer Book introduced into Scotland
1642 Beginning of Civil War
1649 Execution of Charles I
1658 Death of Oliver Cromwell
1662 Royal Society founded
1666 Fire of London

1690 Battle of the Boyne

1707 Act of Union with Scotland

UNIT 1

AIMS

In this unit we will find out about the reign of King Henry VIII (1509 to 1547). We will see how he increased his power over his kingdom of England and Wales and over the Church.

Henry brought great changes to the religious life of England and Wales. We will go on to see how his three children, all of whom became monarchs, also brought changes in religion. We will look at how far these changes affected the lives of the people.

The new monarchy

When Henry VIII became king in 1509 he was just under 18 years old, nearly 2 metres tall, broad-shouldered and athletic. He loved hunting, as Source 1 explains, but was also excellent at archery, wrestling, tennis, bowls and jousting. Jousting was a medieval sport, still popular in the early 16th century: two knights on horseback, carrying wooden lances, would charge at each other and try to knock the other off his horse. Henry made his jousting partner, Charles Brandon, duke of Suffolk. Like many fit men, Henry became fat when he stopped taking exercise as he grew older. Source 2 shows his jousting armour from later in his life. It is 137 cm round the waist.

These physical skills alone would have made Henry popular in the Middle Ages, but by the 16th century people admired other skills as well. Henry was a good musician and composed songs. He was also a friend of some of the cleverest Englishmen of his time, like John Colet and Thomas More.

'His Majesty is 29 years old and extremely handsome. Nature could not have done more for him. On hearing that Francis I (King of France) wore a beard, he allowed his own to grow and as it is reddish, he now has a beard that looks like gold. He is very talented, a good musician, speaks French, Latin and Spanish, is very religious, attends three services a day when he hunts and sometimes five on other days. He is very fond of hunting and sometimes tires out eight or ten horses in a day.'

SOURCE 1
A description of Henry VIII in 1520 by the Venetian ambassador to London.

SOURCE 2
This suit of armour was made for Henry VIII towards the end of his life.

The power of the ruler

In the later Middle Ages several kings were removed from the throne by powerful barons. Some were killed in battle or ASSASSINATED. Henry VIII's father, Henry VII, had only become king by defeating and killing Richard III at the battle of Bosworth in 1485. Henry VII had to work hard to hold on to the throne, especially in the early years of his reign. Henry VIII was determined to be a powerful and respected king. As we shall see in this unit, he increased the power of the monarchy in several ways. For this reason, he is sometimes called a 'New Monarch'.

One aspect of New Monarchy was that monarchs displayed their wealth and power on every possible occasion. Henry VIII's physical abilities and intelligence helped him to do this. He also rivalled other kings in Europe. Source 3 shows a grand meeting he held in 1520 with King Francis I of France just outside Calais called the Field of the Cloth of Gold. He built a huge temporary palace of timber and canvas. Hundreds of pounds worth of velvet, satin and cloth of gold were shipped across to decorate the tents or for attendants' clothes. Francis did the same, and they promised to be allies, a promise that only lasted 18 months.

---

1 Make a list of Henry VIII's skills and abilities. Divide your list into 'Physical' and 'Intellectual'.

2 The sources on these pages have been chosen to give a powerful impression of Henry. Do you think he seems to be:
 a a good king?
 b a nice person?

Think about your own judgement of Henry as you read more about him on the next few pages.

SOURCE 3
A painting of the 'Field of the Cloth of Gold' in 1520 showing some of the prefabricated buildings and many richly-hung tents. You can see Henry and Cardinal Wolsey in the bottom left-hand corner.

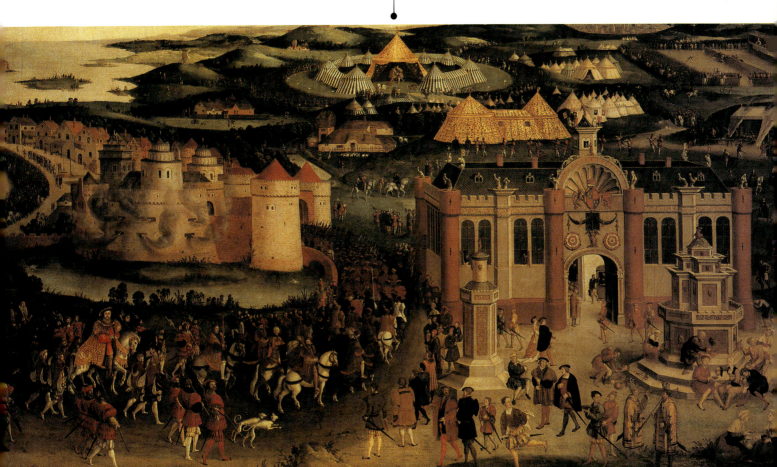

THE NEW MONARCHY

Henry's rule

Henry found the business of governing the country boring. He was happy to leave it to the able men he chose as his chief MINISTERS. These men became very powerful, but fell into disgrace if they failed to deliver what Henry wanted.

Thomas Wolsey was Henry's first minister and held supreme power from 1515 to 1529. Many were jealous of him, but he governed well, as Source 4 shows.

Peace was not really to Henry's liking. Great kings made their names in war. Wars also kept powerful barons busy. Henry went to war with England's old enemy, France, three times in his reign. Scotland, a separate country at this time, usually joined in on France's side. The English inflicted crushing defeats on the Scots at Flodden in 1513 and Solway Moss in 1547. Henry also took a personal interest in building up the navy (see Source 5).

> And for your realm our Lord be thanked that it never was in such peace and TRANQUILLITY. For all this summer I have heard neither of riot, robbery or burglary, but that your laws be in every place administered without leaning of any matter.

SOURCE 4
Extract from a letter written by Wolsey to Henry VIII.

Henry and the Church

Several medieval monarchs had clashed with the Church because it was outside their control. The Pope in Rome was the head of the Church. Henry was loyal to the Pope. He had no sympathy with the attacks on the Pope by Martin Luther, the German founder of PROTESTANTISM. If you look at any British coin you will see, on the 'heads' side, the letters F.D. (or Fid. Def.). These stand for *Fidei Defensor* (Defender of the Faith), a title given to Henry by the Pope in 1521 for writing a book criticising Luther. In 1525 William Tyndale translated the Bible into English. This was against the law and copies had to be smuggled into the country. Henry had those caught doing this executed.

SOURCE 5
The *Mary Rose*. Launched in 1515, the *Mary Rose* had 207 guns and was designed to carry 1,000 soldiers as well as the crew. She sank suddenly off Portsmouth in 1545 when she turned sharply and water entered the gun-ports. Only 30 people survived drowning.

SOURCE 6
Catherine of Aragon.

SOURCE 7
Anne Boleyn.

By the late 1520s, however, Henry's feelings were changing. In 1509 he had married Catherine of Aragon (Source 6), a Spanish princess who had earlier been briefly married to his elder brother Arthur. Henry loved Catherine in the early years of their marriage. However, they only had one daughter, Mary, and Catherine was now too old to have any more children.

Henry felt he had to have a son to be king when he died and he had fallen in love with Anne Boleyn (Source 7), a much younger woman. He therefore wanted to divorce Catherine and marry Anne. For ROMAN CATHOLICS, to this day, the only person who can grant a divorce is the Pope. Wolsey failed to persuade the Pope to agree. He fell from power and died in 1529. In the same year the Pope came under the influence of the Emperor Charles, Catherine's nephew. Charles did not want his aunt removed as queen.

'Mine own sweetheart, this shall be to tell you of my great loneliness that I find here since your departing. For I assure you the time seems longer since your leaving than the last fortnight. I think your kindness and the strength of my love causes it.'

SOURCE 8
Extract from a letter to Anne written by Henry.

ACTIVITY

Do this activity in groups of two or three. There are perhaps four possible solutions to Henry's problem, or 'The King's Great Matter' as it was called:

a Decide that Catherine's marriage to Henry is illegal. Henry can therefore marry Anne.
b Persuade Catherine to become a nun. This would end the marriage and Henry could therefore marry Anne. However, Catherine can only do this voluntarily and she has so far refused.
c Find a reason for delay, hoping the situation will change.
d Decide that Catherine's marriage to Henry is legal and so a divorce is impossible.

1 Some groups are advisers to the Pope. Some are members of Henry's Council. Each group chooses one of the four solutions, or makes up another solution of their own, giving their reasons for choosing their solution and rejecting the others. Exchange views in the whole class.

2 What is your opinion of this extraordinary situation from the point of view of a late 20th-century person? Are there different views between the boys and the girls in your class?

THE NEW MONARCHY

Head of the Church

The job of carrying out what Henry wanted now fell to Thomas Cromwell (Source 9). This clever man made enormous changes to English government and the Church. Most of these changes were carried out through Parliament, so all the leading people in England were involved, and could feel consulted. Working this way also allowed Henry to tell foreigners that it was Parliament that was making these changes, not him. It was Cromwell, however, who managed the Parliament.

Events moved quickly:

- **1532** Parliament made the Church in England agree that Henry was their Head. Anne Boleyn became pregnant.
- **1533** Henry secretly married Anne. Thomas Cranmer became Archbishop of Canterbury and declared that Henry was never legally married to Catherine. Anne Boleyn was crowned Queen.
- **1534** Parliament passed Act of Supremacy, making Henry Supreme Head of the Church in England (see Source 10). Parliament ended payment of taxes to the Pope. Parliament brought in death penalty for anyone refusing to take an oath of loyalty to Henry as Head of the Church.
- **1534** Sir Thomas More (Source 11) was executed for refusing to take the oath.

SOURCE 9
Thomas Cromwell.

'The King's Majesty justly and rightfully is and ought to be the supreme head of the Church in England . . . Yet for confirmation thereof and for increase of Christ's religion in this realm of England, be it enacted by authority of this present Parliament that the King our Sovereign Lord shall be accepted the only Supreme Head of the Church of England.'

SOURCE 10
An extract from the Act of Supremacy, 1534.

SOURCE 11
Thomas More, painted by Holbein.

Discuss your answers to these questions in pairs.

1. How did Thomas Cromwell succeed in solving Henry's problem where Wolsey had failed?
2. What part did Parliament play in these changes?

THE NEW MONARCHY

Dissolution of the Monasteries

Thomas Cromwell also promised to make Henry the richest monarch in Europe. He planned to do this by attacking the monasteries and nunneries. There were 513 monasteries and 130 nunneries in England and Wales. Between them they owned about a quarter of the land. Many people criticised the monks and nuns and were jealous of their wealth. Certainly some abbots lived like rich landowners (see Source 13). A few monks and nuns failed to live up to the strict standards they were supposed to keep. But that had always been so and there is no evidence that things were any worse in the 1530s.

However, all monks and nuns were supposed to be loyal to the Pope, not the king. Thomas Cromwell therefore had two ways of attacking them: for refusing to accept Henry as Head of the Church or for misbehaviour.

In 1535 Cromwell sent visitors to all the monasteries and nunneries looking for these things. He also had a valuation made of their wealth: the *Valor Ecclesiasticus* (see Source 14). In 1536 all religious houses worth less than £200 per year were closed by Act of Parliament: 270 were shut down. The larger houses then surrendered gradually, until by 1539 they had all been suppressed. Monks and nuns were given pensions varying from £50 a year for an abbot to £3 a year for a nun. Hardly anyone resisted, but the abbot of Glastonbury Abbey and two of his monks objected and were executed on Glastonbury Tor. Henry was richer by a million pounds.

> Who is able to count this idle gang who, without working, have got into their hands more than one third of your realm? The best lordships, manors and lands are theirs. Besides this they have the tenth part of all the corn, meadow, pasture, grass, wool, calves, lambs, pigs, geese and chickens. Yes, and they look so carefully at their profits that poor wives must give them every tenth egg, or else she shall be regarded as a heathen.

SOURCE 12
Extract from a book by Simon Fish criticising the Church, published in 1528.

SOURCE 13
Inside the Abbot's House at Muchelney Abbey. This was a rich monastery, worth £447 a year. The monks had been criticised for living too well, riding about the country and neglecting the church.

SOURCE 14
Front page of the *Valor Ecclesiasticus*.

THE NEW MONARCHY

ACTIVITY

Divide the class into six equal groups:

Group 1: Monks from the abbey at Bury St Edmunds (see Source 16).
Group 2: Nuns from the nunnery at Bury St Edmunds (see Source 17).
Group 3: Monks from Richard Beerely's monastery (see Source 18).
Group 4: Monks from Muchelney Abbey (see Source 13).
Group 5: Thomas Cromwell's 'Visitors'. They were chosen by him and knew that he was looking for reasons to close down monasteries and nunneries.
Group 6: People from near the religious houses in Groups 1 to 4. The visitors did not visit everywhere personally, but could take evidence from people living within ten miles. Some local people were in favour of monasteries and nunneries, some were against them.

SOURCE 15
A print showing a nun and monk.

One visitor (Group 5) and one person from Group 6 visits each of Groups 1 to 4. The monks and nuns in these groups must think what to say. Do you want your house to stay open? How are you going to defend yourself? During the visit the visitor keeps notes of what is said. At the end the visitor announces whether the monastery or nunnery is to be closed down.

'We found out nothing bad about the abbot but he often slept in monastic property away from Bury. He loved building beautiful buildings for himself. He increases the rents and shortens the LEASES of poor people who rent land from the monastery. He also keeps on with Roman Catholic CEREMONIES.'

SOURCE 16
Extract from the report of John ap Rice, Visitor to the abbey at Bury St Edmunds, to Thomas Cromwell, November 1535.

'I could not find out anything bad about the nunnery no matter how hard I tried. I believe that everybody had got together and agreed to keep things secret. Eight of the nuns will leave because they are under age. Five others would like to depart if possible.'

SOURCE 17
Extract from the report of John ap Rice, Visitor to the nunnery at Bury St Edmunds, to Thomas Cromwell, November 1535.

My lowly and meek scribbling to your noble Grace at this time comes from my worry that the religion which we keep is no rule of St Benedict . . . The monks here have taken little notice of King Henry's command that any mention of the Pope should be crossed out of all our books. The monks drink and play bowls after breakfast until 10 o'clock or midday. They come to morning service drunk. They do nothing for the love of God. They have many other faults which I have no time to tell you about.

SOURCE 18
Extract from a letter written in 1535 to Thomas Cromwell by Richard Beerely, a monk.

THE NEW MONARCHY

Increasing royal power

With Henry as Supreme Head, the separate power of the Church was now ended. But royal control was still weak in certain parts of England and Wales.

The North

In 1536 there was a protest against the Dissolution of the Monasteries in the North, led by Robert Aske and called the Pilgrimage of Grace (see Source 19). It was crushed, but Thomas Cromwell set about increasing royal control over the North, both to prevent further rebellions and to weaken the powerful northern barons. The Council of the North, meeting in York, already existed, but was strengthened and filled with Henry's officials.

SOURCE 19
Banner carried by rebels in the 'Pilgrimage of Grace', 1536.

Wales

Edward I had conquered Wales in 1282, defeating the last independent Welsh prince and seizing his lands. Henry VII was the son of a Welshman, Edmund Tudor, and had become king in 1485 with Welsh support. Nevertheless, large parts of Wales were still ruled by marcher lords, who claimed to be independent of royal laws. Lawlessness was common.

Thomas Cromwell first appointed Rowland Lee, Bishop of Lichfield, to sort this problem out. Lee hated the Welsh and had 5,000 of them hanged. He also insisted on the Welsh using surnames, like the English did. Many Welsh names thus became Anglicised. For example, Ap Rhys (son of Rhys) became Price, Coch (Red) became Gooch or Gough and many children of Sion became Jones.

Then Cromwell made Parliament pass a series of Acts of Union between 1536 and 1543. These Acts set up a local system of law and order with separate counties (see Source 20) and Justices of the Peace, exactly as in England. Each Welsh county sent one Member of Parliament (MP) to Parliament. English law and the English language were to be used. The Acts brought law and order, as well as other benefits, but only if the Welsh abandoned some of their Welshness.

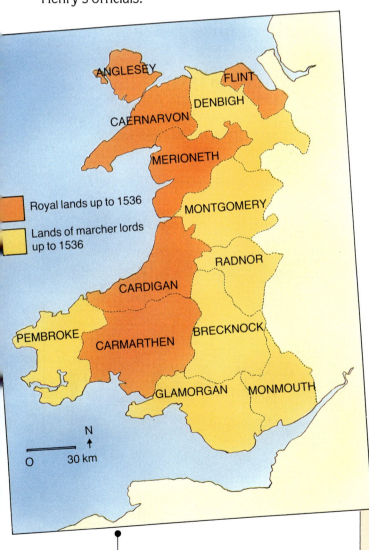

SOURCE 20
Map showing the counties of Wales created by the Act of Union 1536. These counties lasted until 1974.

Discuss this question in pairs.

What did the following gain or lose by the Acts of Union of 1536 to 1543?
a The Welsh people.
b The English government.

THE NEW MONARCHY

The Reformation in England and Wales

By the 1530s Europe was torn by arguments and wars over religion. Those who wanted change protested at the Roman Catholic Church and so were called Protestants. They wanted to reform [change] their churches, so these changes are called the Reformation.

Reformation from above

Most people at that time expected their ruler to decide what their religion should be. If the ruler changed, and new ideas were brought in, most people accepted them. The early years of the Reformation in this country therefore were years of Reformation from above.

Henry VIII

Henry, like most of his people, was always a Roman Catholic at heart. He had made himself Head of the Church (see page 10) to get his divorce, but churches and church services stayed the same (see Source 22). Some of his ministers were in favour of Protestant ideas. Cromwell and Archbishop Cranmer persuaded him in 1537 to have the Bible in English placed in every church. Henry backtracked even on this, and in 1543 made it an offence to read the Bible out loud to another person.

Edward VI (1547 to 1553)

Edward was Henry's only son. Although he was only nine years old when he became king, Edward was a keen Protestant. He worked with

> '1547 Jake Ball and Richard Boonde bought the silver and gold plate (used in the Roman Catholic Service). We received £15–6s (£15.30).
> 1548 We have whitewashed the walls of our chancel. We paid 3/- (15p).
> 1549 Robert Halle has made a trestle table for us and put it up in the chancel. He has removed the high stone altar. We paid 2d (1p). We have bought two new Service books in English. We paid out 7/4 (37p). Betts of Wetherden removed the organ. We paid 5/4 (27p).
> 1550 We bought Cranmer's New Prayer Book. We paid 20d (8p).'

SOURCE 21 Extracts from the CHURCHWARDEN's accounts from St Mary's Church, Boxford, Suffolk.

SOURCE 22 Inside a Roman Catholic church.

1 Rood beam
2 Cross
3 Service book in Latin
4 Priest
5 Altar
6 Candles
7 Statue of Virgin Mary
8 Stained glass windows
9 Nave (where the people worshipped)

THE NEW MONARCHY

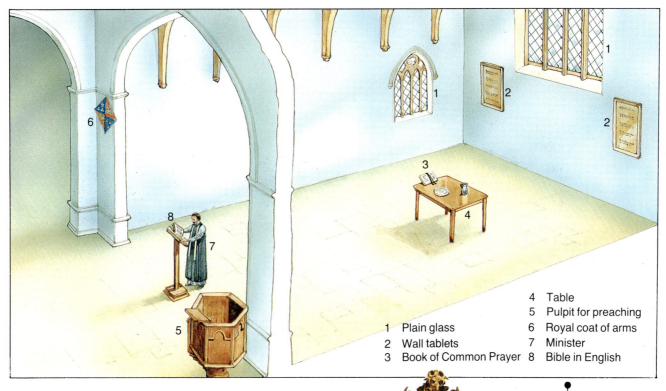

1	Plain glass	4	Table
2	Wall tablets	5	Pulpit for preaching
3	Book of Common Prayer	6	Royal coat of arms
		7	Minister
		8	Bible in English

SOURCE 23
Inside a Protestant church.

SOURCE 24
Medieval wood-carving of the Virgin and Child. Thousands of carvings like this were burnt by the Protestant reformers.

Archbishop Cranmer to bring in the Protestant Reformation. A new Prayer Book, in English, was issued in 1549, and another one, even more different from Roman Catholic ways, in 1552. Local people were ordered to change their churches as well (see Source 21). Protestants felt it was wrong to have pictures, statues and finely dressed priests. They wanted plain churches (see Source 23) and services in English so that they could be understood.

These changes upset many people. Many old traditions, such as local saints, Church ales, Plough Monday, holly and ivy at Christmas and tolling the church bell for the dead, were swept away. People in Devon objected so much to these changes that they rebelled (see Source 25).

SOURCE 25
Some of the demands of the rebels in the Devon Prayer Book rebellion of 1549.

'We will have statues set up again in every church and all other ceremonies used until now by our mother the holy Church . . . We will not receive the new service because it is like a Christmas game but we will have our old service in Latin as it was before, not in English.'

attainment target

1. What differences are there between the church in Source 22 and the one in Source 23?
2. What changes would you have noticed in Boxford Church if you had gone there every Sunday between 1547 and 1550?
3. How would the work of the churchwardens at Boxford be regarded by
   a Cranmer, and
   b the Devon Prayer Book rebels?

SOURCE 26
A painting of Henry VIII and his children. This is not a real scene, but is trying to give a message. Henry VIII sits in the centre with his son, Edward, kneeling before him. To the left is Mary, with her husband, King Philip of Spain, and the god of war. To the right is Elizabeth with the goddesses of peace and plenty trampling on the weapons of war.

Mary (1553 to 1558)

Mary was the daughter of Catherine of Aragon. She had been deeply affected by her mother's divorce and was determined to make England Roman Catholic again. Churches began to be changed back once more (Source 27).

There were actually very few Protestants in England at this time. In some places there was a tradition of Lollardy, which came from the 14th-century followers of John Wyclif. Protestant ideas were strongest in South-East England. This was the most properous area of the country and in closest contact with Protestants in Holland and Germany. About 800 Protestants fled abroad when Mary came to the throne.

From 1555 onwards Mary began to use the fiercest punishment of the law on Protestants who refused to become Catholics: they were burnt alive (see Source 29). Archbishop Cranmer was burnt, and four other bishops, but the statistics of the 280 people burnt show where Protestant support lay:

- 193 were burnt in London, Kent, Essex, Suffolk, Norfolk and Sussex.
- 1 in the North (Chester), 1 in the West (Exeter), 3 in Wales.
- 55 women were burnt.

'**1554** We bought a Mass book (Roman Catholic service) from London. We paid 13/8 (67p). We bought a COPE and new VESTMENTS (for the priest to wear). We paid 10/- (50p).
1555 The glazier from Hadleigh replaced some of our stained glass. 5/- (25p).
1556 To mend a cloth for the altar 2d (1p) Hartewell has put up an iron rail around the altar. We paid 5/- (25p).
1557 Childerley buys INCENSE for us. 2d (1p) New statues and paintings are put up. 20/- (£1)'

SOURCE 27
Extracts from the churchwarden's accounts of St Mary's, Boxford, Suffolk.

THE NEW MONARCHY

Elizabeth (1558 to 1603)

Elizabeth was Anne Boleyn's daughter, connected since her birth with the break from the Pope. She could see how useful it was to be Head of the Church, and had moderate Protestant ideas. In 1559 she turned the country back to being Protestant again, more or less as it had been in the middle of Edward's reign (Source 28).

Religion and the people

So where did all these changes leave the people of England and Wales? We have seen that in Henry VIII's time most people were Roman Catholics. By the middle of Elizabeth's reign their sons and daughters were mostly Protestants. The new religion appealed to the new generation who were not so attached to the old ways. Keen Protestant preachers worked hard to persuade them. Many people were horrified at the burnings of Mary's reign. Foxe's *Book of Martyrs* was published in 1563 and even those who could not read it could understand the lurid pictures (see Source 29). William Morgan's Bible in Welsh, published in 1588, helped Protestants to spread their ideas in Wales. Devon, base of the anti-Protestant rebellion of 1549, became the breeding-ground of Protestant sailors like Francis Drake.

Puritans and Catholics

But the religious unity of the country was broken. There were some extreme Protestants, called Puritans, for whom Elizabeth did not go nearly far enough. They wanted to 'purify' the Church of any part of Roman Catholicism which still remained. They were opposed to bishops and chose their own ministers. Puritans took more part in church services, especially singing hymns.

There were also Roman Catholics. Elizabeth was a tolerant person, and her own organist, William Byrd, was a Catholic. Some Catholics went to church because they had to. John Trevelyan, a Cornish Catholic landowner, would always leave before the sermon, calling out to the priest 'When you have finished what you have to say, come and have dinner with me.'

Roman Catholic priests such as Edmund Campion were sent to England. For most of Elizabeth's reign Roman Catholicism's main supporter was Spain, England's arch-enemy. With England at war with Catholic Spain, the government thought that these priests were spies. Campion was arrested, tortured and executed.

'1559 We have bought the new Prayer Book. We paid 5/- (25p). Roland has pulled down the altar. We paid 10d (4p). To pay for pulling down the rood loft 6/8 (33p) Lynche has made us a communion table 2/- (10p). To remove stained glass and replace it with plain glass 10/- (50p).'

SOURCE 28
Extract from the churchwarden's accounts of St Mary's, Boxford, Suffolk.

SOURCE 29
An illustration from Foxe's *Book of Martyrs* showing the burning of Thomas Hawkes, at Coggeshall, Essex, in 1555.

attainment target

1. Use Sources 27 and 28 to explain what was changed, and what remained the same in Boxford Church in the years 1554 to 1559.

2. Do you think that by 1559, after all the changes, Boxford church looked like a Catholic church or a Protestant church?

3. The 25 years from the time when Henry VIII became Head of the Church marked great changes in religion in England. In which five-year period did religion change a lot and in which five years did religion hardly change at all? Explain your answer.

4. What do you think were the most important changes in these 25 years from the point of view of: the monarch; the people of Boxford; Roman Catholics?

UNIT 2

People and homes

Montacute House, Somerset (Source 1), was begun in about 1590. It was built in the latest style. If you compare it with Cothay Manor (Source 2), built in 1480, you can see just how much styles had changed.

The rooms inside were different too. Cothay Manor has a great hall where all the family and servants met and ate together; Montacute has more private rooms. Montacute has a 'parlour', a room for sitting and talking with friends, from the French *parler* (to speak). It also has gardens, perhaps with some of the new flowers brought into England in the 17th century: tulips, from Turkey; sunflowers, from Peru; and nasturtiums, from America. If the weather was wet, family and guests could exercise in the Long Gallery (Source 3).

AIMS

In this unit we will find out more about the people of England and Wales, and how they lived. We will discover who was doing well, like the owners of the houses on these pages, and who was not. We will also see how difficult it is to find accurate information about people at this time.

SOURCE 1
Montacute House, Somerset.

SOURCE 2
Cothay Manor, Somerset.

SOURCE 3
The Long Gallery at Montacute House.

The great rebuilding

Montacute House was built by Edward Phelips. The Dissolution of the Monasteries had meant lots of buying and selling of land. Phelips was a lawyer and had become rich by arranging these deals. He built Montacute to display his wealth.

All over England, in the years 1540 to 1640, some people were doing well and building themselves new houses. One historian has called this period 'the great rebuilding'. Successful farmers built themselves new farmhouses. Local gentry families in particular did well, often from the profits of former monastic land.

Compare Montacute House (Source 1) with Cothay Manor (Source 2). What are the differences? You could think about: size, height, size of windows, and symmetry.

SOURCE 4
Painting showing Queen Elizabeth I being carried to a wedding in June 1600.

'We in England divide our people into four groups: First there are the gentlemen. After the monarch, the first gentlemen are the lords and noblemen. After them are squires, simply called gentlemen. Second come citizens, freemen who live in the cities. Third come the yeomen. They are those who own a certain amount of land. The fourth and last group are day labourers, farmworkers, shopkeepers who have no land, and all craftsmen, such as tailors, shoemakers, carpenters, bricklayers, etc.'

SOURCE 5
Adapted from a book written by William Harrison and published in 1586.

Who were the people of England and Wales at this time? One writer, William Harrison, divided them into four groups (Source 5). Today we want better information than just a description: we want statistics. In the 16th and 17th centuries there were no government officials to collect statistics. No one thought it necessary. In the late 17th century Gregory King made rough estimates of the number of people in each group. Source 6 is a summary of his figures.

Distinctions between these groups were very strict. In the 1630s a man who said he was a better man than the Earl of Danby was put in prison and fined £2,000. There were also laws about the clothes you could wear. No one under the rank of baron could wear silver, satin or red velvet, and if a labourer wore cloth that cost more than 10d (4p) a yard, he could be put in the STOCKS for three days.

	Size of household	Total numbers	Income per year
• Gentlemen: lords, noblemen	16–40	20,000	£5,000–£800
Gentlemen: squires	8–15	134,000	£800–£300
• Citizens	5–8	250,000	£300–£100
• Yeomen	5–7	1,660,000	£100–£40
• Labourers, etc.	2–4	3,250,000	£40–£7
Vagrants, beggars, etc.	–	30,000	–

SOURCE 6
Summary of Gregory King's estimates of the people of England, published in 1696.

PEOPLE AND HOMES

Gentlemen

Nobles, lords and the richest gentlemen spent much of their time at court, with the monarch. In Source 4, Elizabeth is not being carried by servants, but by noblemen. Attendance at court was extremely expensive. You were expected to make a great show, and employ lots of servants.

When the Queen travelled about, she, and all her followers, stayed at a lord's house. This could be a great honour. If she did come, the royal party would consume as much food in a day as was normally eaten in a month.

Gentlemen like Sir Henry Tichborne (Source 8) rarely, if ever, went to court. They stayed at home and played a large part in running their county. Many became Justices of the Peace (JPs) who not only tried criminals, but fixed wages and prices. As Source 8 shows, they were like local kings. In Wales, too, farming was doing well, and the new JPs (see page 13) lived like English gentlemen.

SOURCE 8
Sir Henry Tichborne handing out bread to his household, tenants and labourers, outside his house in Hampshire.

> Parts of Wales were 'rough all over and unpleasant to see, with craggy stones, hanging rocks and ragged ways'. Elsewhere the fields were well looked after 'in some places barley, in others wheat, but generally throughout rye and afterwards four or five crops together of oats'.

SOURCE 7
Extract from *Britannia*, written by William Camden in 1586.

---

1. Describe the clothes worn by the people in Source 4.
2. Do you think a nobleman would think it an honour, or a disgrace, to carry the queen in this way?
3. Why do you think the queen had this painting (Source 4) made? What did she want people to think about her? What did she want people to think about the nobles?
4. Why do you think Sir Henry Tichborne had Source 8 painted?

PEOPLE AND HOMES

Merchants

The second group in Harrison's list (Source 5) were citizens. By 1600 perhaps one-fifth of the population of England lived in towns. London was by far the biggest, with probably 200,000 people. Norwich was next with 17,000, then York and Bristol with about 10,000 each.

In the Middle Ages the South-East of England had been much richer than the North and West. Now those areas were catching up. Totnes, Plymouth and Exeter were growing because of the cloth trade. Poole was an important port, and Newcastle was sending coal to London. Birmingham was starting to grow 'echoing with the noise of ANVILS', as William Camden put it. Leeds, Halifax and Manchester were prospering and Sheffield was becoming famous for cutlery.

Trade was still far less important than agriculture, but it was growing steadily. As more people travelled on business they needed better places to stay, to leave their horses and talk to customers. Many fine inns were built at this time, like the Feathers at Ludlow (Source 9).

Rich merchants contributed to the great rebuilding of England by building large town houses (Source 11). One such rich merchant was William Marritt of Lincoln, who died in 1616. When he died a careful list, called an inventory, was made of everything in his house. It gives us an interesting look at how he lived and furnished his house.

Source 13 shows the actual text of the inventory for one of the rooms. Source 12 gives more of the inventory and Source 10 is a plan to help you find your way round Marritt's house.

SOURCE 9
A 16th-century inn, The Feathers, at Ludlow, Shropshire.

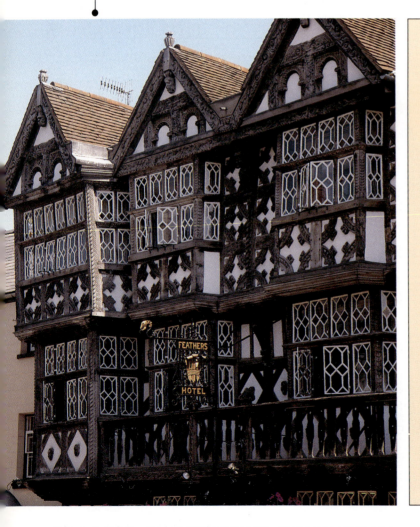

attainment target

Read Source 12 carefully.

1. What was each of the six rooms described mainly used for?

2. How useful is Source 12 for telling us about
   a. What goods he traded in?
   b. How well-off he was?
   c. What he was like?
   d. Anything else about 17th-century England?

3. Look back at Source 6. What would you want to know about Gregory King in order to assess how reliable this source is?

4. King's figures may be wrong. Do you think we should ignore Source 6 entirely? Explain your answer.

5. Copy out this table and comment on how useful the four sources are for finding out about the people of England at this time:

	Advantages	Disadvantages
Source 5		
Source 6		
Source 8		
Source 12		

PEOPLE AND HOMES

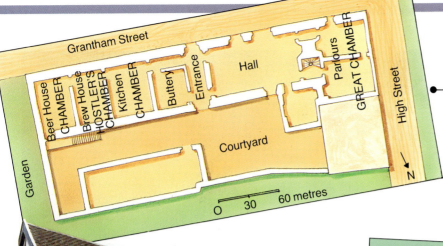

SOURCE 10
Plan of William Marritt's house. The upstairs rooms are labelled in capital letters.

SOURCE 11
William Marritt's house today.

In the parlour next the street wherein he lodged. Firstly his purse, his gown, two cloaks and his other clothes – £12. Also one bedstead, one featherbed, *bolster* and other bedding and curtains for that bed – £4. Two joined chests, one trunk, one desk and other implements 23s 4d (£1.17p). Total £17.17.

In the buttery
One hundred and two pounds of *pewter*, of pan metal thirty eight pounds, of brass candlesticks twenty pounds, six dishes, one bed pan, one *press*, two old *hutches*.

In the kitchen
Two dressers, three dripping pans, five spits, hooks.

In the brewhouse
Brewing tubs, barrels and other implements.

In the great chamber
One long table and three trestles, two bedsteads, two featherbeds, two green rugs, two pairs of curtains, two truckle bedsteads, two featherbeds, three pairs of blankets, two coverings. One square table, two chairs, one chest, six leather cushions, one other chest, one *close-stool*, twenty four pairs of sheets, six dozen napkins, twenty three pillowcases, eight table cloths, thirteen towels.

In the chamber over the kitchen
Three servant bedsteads, bedding, chairs and other furniture.

Bolster: a large pillow.
Pewter: a metal made of tin and lead, used for cups, plates, etc.
Press: for making cheese
Hutch: cupboards
Close-stool: toilet, like a commode.
The chambers were upstairs rooms.

SOURCE 12
Modern transcript of some of the inventory. (The value of items is given for the first room only.)

SOURCE 13
Part of a page of the inventory of William Marritt.

PEOPLE AND HOMES

SOURCE 14
Farm in the Lake District, dated 1629.

Yeomen

Yeomen were farmers who owned their own small farm or paid a fixed, low rent for their holding. The population of England and Wales was rising, so food prices were high and farmers did well. Their increased wealth can be seen in the many new farmhouses built between 1540 and 1640. The Lake District farmhouse in Source 14 may not look very grand, but it is solid, with glass in the windows and stone chimneys. The demand for food helped Welsh cattle farmers too. They drove their animals hundreds of miles from the Welsh hills to English markets. Welsh cattle drovers became rich and set up some of the first banks in Wales.

Yeomen farmers improved their standard of living in various other ways, as Source 16 suggests. Source 15 may be an exaggeration, but even if he was better off than a gentleman, a yeoman of Kent would always regard the gentleman as his superior.

> There are old men still dwelling in the village where I live who have noted three things to be marvellously altered in England in their memory; the multitude of chimneys lately erected; the great improvement of beds . . . for we used to lie on straw sacks with a good round log for a pillow . . . and the change of vessels of wood into pewter.

SOURCE 15
A 16th-century rhyme.

*A knight of Cales (Calais)
A gentlemen of Hailes
A laird of the North Countree
A yeoman of Kent,
Sitting on his penny rent,
Could buy them out all three.*

SOURCE 16
An extract from a book by William Harrison, published in 1586.

PEOPLE AND HOMES

Labourers

On the whole labourers (the largest group in Source 5) were not doing very well at this time. Wages in towns were low: 1d a day for apprentice weavers, 2d a day for blacksmiths, 4d a day for master carpenters, although they often received food as well. In those days beef cost 2d a pound and a pair of shoes up to 1/- (5p).

Farmworkers toiled for long hours in the fields: 11½ hours was normal at harvest time. Their wages went up only slowly, while food prices rose quickly. Sources 18 and 19 may give rather too rosy an impression of a labourer's lifestyle.

SOURCE 17
Pewter candlestick.

SOURCE 18
Inside a labourer's cottage.

SOURCE 19
Inventory of Thomas Hearne. He was quite comfortably off although only a farmworker.

In the Hall
A table, a bench, a plank, two chairs, two shelves and painted cloths.
Brass: one pot, three kettles, two pans, a basin, two candlesticks.
Pewter: four plates, two bowls, a salt cellar, a saucer.
A bowl, a pair of bellows, dishes.

Chamber
An old bedstead, a cupboard, an old chest and painted cloths. Apples worth 10/- (50p). An axe, a hatchet, a wedge, a *billhook*, a spit, a pair of *andirons* and pot-hangers.

Chamber in the entry (on the landing?)
A plain bedstead, a flocked bolster and a coverlet. An old bedstead, a chest and a tub.

Kitchen
A tub, three boards, two spinning wheels, a grindstone and pot-hangers.

Barn
Wheat and barley worth £4.15 (£4.75p). Hay and feed worth £1.
Ladders, sieves and other lumber. One cow and two young bullocks worth £2.10.
Crops in the ground this year worth £1.10 (£1.50p).

Billhook: a curved knife on a pole.
Andirons: for holding logs in a fireplace.

ACTIVITY

Look at Source 19. Working in pairs, make sure you understand what everything in the inventory is, what it looked like and how it was used. Use a dictionary and the library to help you.

1 Try to draw a room in Thomas Hearne's house, or imagine Thomas or his wife showing you around their cottage. Remember that every single thing of value they had is in the inventory.

2 What can you tell from this inventory about the life of Thomas Hearne and his wife? What would it be like to live there? Remember that although they are among the better-off farmworkers in the village, many yeomen and gentlemen were far richer. Remember also that Thomas and his wife accepted this as the way things were.

3 Act out, or write, some episodes in a day in the life of Thomas Hearne and his wife.

PEOPLE AND HOMES

SOURCE 20
Hardwick Hall.

SOURCE 21
Elizabeth, Countess of Shrewsbury, 'Bess of Hardwick'.

'The paradise of married women'

It was not just men who built houses to show off their wealth. Source 20 shows the front of Hardwick Hall in Derbyshire, one of the most spectacular Elizabethan houses in England, begun in 1591. The letters E S round the roof stand for Elizabeth, Countess of Shrewsbury (Source 21), who had it built. She had become very rich as a result of four marriages to wealthy men, who left their money to her when they died.

'Bess of Hardwick' as she was called, was hardly typical. What was life really like for women in the period 1540 to 1640? A Dutchman who knew England well described the lives of women that he saw, and called England 'A paradise of married

PEOPLE AND HOMES

women' (see Source 22). The other sources on these pages will help you decide if he was right.

As with men, the lives of women depended very much on how rich they were. Poorer women were expected to work hard at their own tasks and help their husbands too – see Source 23 and also Source 18 (page 25).

Working women obviously made important contributions to the survival of the family, both working alongside their husbands and on their own.

One task which always fell to women was caring for people in times of crisis, such as childbirth, death or illness. Only rich people used doctors. Women in the village passed round recipes for medicines and cures. They had practical skills, especially in midwifery (Source 25) which were essential.

> Wives in England are entirely in the power of their husbands, yet they are not kept so strictly as in Spain. Nor are they shut up . . . They go to market to buy what they like best to eat. They are well-dressed, fond of taking it easy and leave the care of the household to their STEWARDS. They sit in front of their doors, dressed in fine clothes, to see and be seen by passers-by. In all banquets and feasts they are shown the highest honour . . . All the rest of the time they spend in walking and riding, in playing at cards, in visiting their friends, conversing with their neighbours and making merry with them and childbirths and christenings. And all this with the permission of their husbands. This is why England is called the paradise of married women.

SOURCE 22
Extract from a book published in 1575 and written by a Dutch merchant, Van Meteren, living in London.

SOURCE 23
Extract from a book about farming, written by Anthony FitzHerbert in 1523.

'It is a wife's occupation to winnow corn, make malt, make hay, and in time of need to help her husband to fill the muck wagon, drive the plough, load hay or corn . . . to go to market to sell butter, cheese, milk, eggs, hens, geese.'

'Took horse and rode to Harwoodall to see our farm be bought . . . I walked with Mr Hoby about the town to spy out the best places where cottages might be built . . . After supper I talked a good deal with Mr Hoby of farming and household matters.'

SOURCE 24
Extract from the diary of Lady Hoby.

SOURCE 25
Midwife attending at childbirth.

> **attainment target**
>
> 1 Do you agree that the life described in Source 22 is 'a paradise for married women'?
>
> 2 What are the advantages and disadvantages of using a description written by a foreign observer? Do you think we are dealing here with facts or opinions?
>
> 3 How much do the following sources support or contradict Van Meteren's views: Source 18, 20, 23, 24 and 25.
>
> 4 Which of these sources might Van Meteren have chosen to support his view?
>
> 5 Do you think England at this time was 'the paradise of married women'?

PEOPLE AND HOMES

SOURCE 26
Begging in London today.

Beggars and vagabonds

What do members of your class feel about people begging, as in Source 26? Our reactions are usually divided between those who think beggars should be made to find work, and those who think they should be helped by the government. The same problems, and the same suggestions for answers, could be found in England 400 years ago.

At that time the number of people who were poor and out of work seemed to be increasing. Some turned to begging, some to crime. There was no unemployment benefit, but people who were disabled and so could not work were allowed to beg. Those who could work and didn't were called vagabonds, and punished. In 1572 the law was toughened up: vagabonds were to be whipped and burned through the gristle of the right ear. This was frequently carried out (see Source 28). The government did this for two reasons:

- They believed that not working was wicked and sinful.
- They were worried about law and order. There was no police force and gangs of vagabonds could do as they pleased.

SOURCE 27
A beggar and a gentleman: an illustration of 1569.

'29 March 1573. At Harrow Hill in Middlesex, John Allan, Elizabeth Turner, Humphrey Foxe, Henry Bower and Agnes Vat, being over 14 years of age and having no lawful means of livelihood, were declared vagabonds. Sentenced to be FLOGGED and burnt through the right ear.'

SOURCE 28
An item from the records of Middlesex, dated 1573.

The rise in unemployment

People at the time blamed many things for the rising numbers of unemployed people: gambling, overspending by the rich, wars with Spain or the Dissolution of the Monasteries which used to look after beggars and vagabonds. Most of all they blamed ENCLOSURES. The growth of the cloth trade meant that sheep farming was profitable. Some landowners stopped arable farming (Source 29) and turned their farms into sheep-walks (Source 30). A comparison of the two pictures shows what effect this had on the number of people employed.

PEOPLE AND HOMES

We have already seen that there were no accurate statistics. Modern historians have pointed out that enclosure for sheep farming actually declined in the late 16th century. They also say that the population was rising fast, so there simply was not enough work for everyone.

The Elizabethan Poor Law

By the end of the 16th century it was clear that harsh laws were not stopping vagabonds. The situation was worst in towns. Some of them, such as Ipswich (Source 31), had a different attitude. Eventually the government passed the great Poor Law of 1601, which lasted until 1834. This said:

- Poor people had to stay in their own parish and not wander about.
- Each parish must look after its own poor, and could collect a local tax, the poor rate, to do this.
- Disabled poor would be looked after in their own houses, out of the poor rate.
- Able-bodied poor would be looked after, but would be given work to do.
- Poor children would also be looked after and taught a trade.

The 1601 Poor Law was quite a change. It seemed to accept that it was not the people's fault if they were poor. It raised money from more fortunate people to look after the poor, in different ways.

SOURCE 29
A 16th-century illustration of harvesting.

SOURCE 30
A 16th-century illustration of a sheep-walk.

'Wednesday, 2 December 1551. Two in every parish shall be nominated by the bailiffs to enquire into the poor of the parish.

Monday, 22 February 1557. No children of this town shall be permitted to beg. Those adults that shall be permitted to beg shall have badges.

Monday, 26 September 1569. The late house of Blackfriars, bought of John Southwell, shall be henceforth a hospital for the poor people of this town and shall be called Christ's Hospital.'

SOURCE 31
Extracts from Ipswich town records.

Discuss your answers to these questions in groups of four.

1. Look at Source 26. What are your views on begging? Do you give money to beggars? Should the government help these people?

2. What are the similarities and differences between the situations in Sources 26 and 27?

3. What were the attitudes of the government to the problems of the poor
   a in 1572?
   b in 1601?

4. How do these attitudes compare with those of the government today?

UNIT 3

Kings and Parliaments

King James VI of Scotland became King James I of England in 1603. As he travelled south to London he was welcomed by the English. Yet only 39 years later the people of Britain were divided by a terrible civil war. At the end of this civil war, James's son Charles was executed for having caused it. What went wrong? How did the joy and unity of 1603 turn into the bitterness and bloodshed of 1642?

AIMS

A civil war is a war between different groups inside a country. In this unit you will discover what went wrong in England to cause the outbreak of the CIVIL WAR in 1642. You will know by now that complex events usually have several causes. Some historians think that the long-term causes of the Civil War go back at least to 1603, perhaps earlier. You will find out about these long-term causes, as well as the short-term causes in the years up to 1642. The unit ends by looking at who won the Civil War and why.

SOURCE 1
James in 1595, aged 29.

SOURCE 2
The execution of Charles I in 1649, from a print made at the time.

Two kingdoms, one king

James was King of England and Scotland. The two countries continued to be separate, as they had been for centuries, linked only by having the same king. One Englishman hated this and said it was like being tied to a dead body and thrown into a ditch. James wanted to unite the two kingdoms but Parliament refused. Nevertheless, as we shall see, England and Scotland did draw closer together over the 17th century.

The Gunpowder Plot 1605

To Roman Catholics, James, a Protestant, was not the rightful king. A group of them plotted to kill him, and many lords and MPs, by blowing up the Houses of Parliament. James's ministers may have known about the plot and used it to stir up anti-Catholic feeling. They waited until they could catch all the plotters, then, on 5 November 1605, Guy Fawkes was arrested and the plot revealed.

Coming after the burning of Protestants in Mary's reign, and the attempted invasion of England by the Spanish Armada in 1588, the Gunpowder Plot increased hatred and fear of Roman Catholics. After 1688 (see unit 4) 5 November was celebrated as Guy Fawkes night. In some places (see Source 4) this has remained an anti-Catholic celebration right up to this century.

SOURCE 3
The Gunpowder Plotters.

SOURCE 4
Guy Fawkes Night in Lewes, Sussex.

1. In 1603 James had already been a successful king of Scotland for 36 years. Do you think this was an advantage or a disadvantage to him in becoming King of England?
2. Why do you think the Gunpowder Plot helped James become more popular?

KINGS AND PARLIAMENTS

The Divine Right of Kings

The Scottish lords had not been easy to rule, so James emphasised royal power. He said that monarchs were chosen by God to govern and could do what they liked or needed to do. This idea was called the Divine Right of Kings (see Source 5). James and his son, Charles, used the best ARCHITECTS and artists of their time to support this view of royal power, as Sources 6 and 7 show.

As we saw in unit 1, in Henry VIII's time most people accepted the idea of an all-powerful monarch. The trouble was that England had changed since then. Misunderstandings and disagreements grew up between James and his people. The main issues were *religion*, *Parliament* and *money*.

> It is not lawful to argue with the King's power. It is contempt in a subject to say that a King cannot do this or that. Kings are the makers of laws . . . and as the King is overlord of the whole land so he has power of life and death over every person that lives in the same.

SOURCE 5
James's idea of monarchy, from a book he wrote in 1603.

Discuss these questions in pairs.
1. How do you react to James's views on the Divine Right of Kings in Source 5?
2. Give three words which describe the interior of the Banqueting House (Sources 6 and 7).
3. How does the design of the Banqueting House build up the power and dignity of the king?

SOURCE 6
Inside the Banqueting House in Whitehall, designed by Inigo Jones in 1619. James met important visitors here, sitting in state.

SOURCE 7
Huge ceiling painting by Rubens in the Banqueting House. It shows James being lifted up to Heaven.

Religion

The Puritans wanted to make England more Protestant than Elizabeth had allowed (see unit 1). They believed that every person had his or her own relationship with God so there was no need for bishops or priests. Scotland was a very Puritan country, so they had high hopes that James would change things. In fact James hated the Puritans of Scotland because they had tried to tell him what to do. He supported bishops and told the Puritans they must accept this or he would 'harry them out of the land'. Some Puritans did leave, such as the Pilgrim Fathers who went to North America in 1620, but many stayed and resented James's attitude.

Parliament

Unlike Scotland where the barons were still important, the most important people in England were the country gentlemen. They ran affairs in their counties and met in the House of Commons. The Scottish Parliament was weak, but the English Parliament, especially the House of Commons, had gradually increased its power. Members of Parliament had been consulted about all the great religious changes of the 16th century. They met more often. The taxes they could grant to the monarch became more and more necessary (see next page). In some of her Parliaments MPs had disagreed with Elizabeth. However, Elizabeth had generally taken note of their views and was trusted by them as a result.

James made little effort to consult them or win their trust. He could hardly believe they would dare to criticise him (see Source 8). He pointed out, quite correctly, that monarchs had the right to call and dismiss Parliaments as they pleased. His response to criticism was to lecture them about Divine Right, on which he considered himself an expert.

James preferred to work with his personal favourites. The most powerful of these was the Duke of Buckingham, or 'Steenie' as James called him. From 1618 to 1628 Steenie really ruled England alongside James and Charles. Some of the many honours and titles he was given are listed next to his portrait (Source 9).

SOURCE 9
George Villiers, Duke, Marquis and Earl of Buckingham, Earl of Coventry, Viscount Villiers, Baron of Whadden, Great Admiral of the kingdom of England and Ireland.

'At their meetings nothing is heard but cries, shouts and confusion. I am surprised that my ANCESTORS should have allowed such an institution to come into existence.'

SOURCE 8
James's views on the House of Commons.

KINGS AND PARLIAMENTS

Money

England was a richer country than Scotland, so James thought that he would be better off when he became king. In fact royal income had risen in value only three times since the 1530s, from £200,000 to £600,000 a year, while prices had risen five or six times. The money from the Dissolution of the Monasteries had been spent on wars and the monastic lands sold off to raise money. Parliament could have granted James more money from taxes, but was reluctant to do so.

James spent money on himself, his family, his friends and on grand entertainment, at a great rate. His household cost £35,000 a year to run, while Elizabeth's had cost only £9,500. Buckingham's foreign wars proved expensive. To make ends meet, James found other sources of income. He had the right to grant titles, so he invented a new one – baronet – and sold it at £1,000 each.

He also had the right to grant monopolies, which was the exclusive right to sell certain goods. Monopolies put up prices and annoyed other traders. James sold over 100 monopolies, including bricks, coal, butter, currants, herrings, tobacco, dice, coaches, hay, belts, buttons, even mousetraps.

Charles I

Charles I (Source 10) was a quiet, mild, but obstinate man. He was a firm believer in the Divine Right of Kings, and had much the same views as his father on Parliament.

> ## ACTIVITY
>
> Get into groups of three or four for this activity, which is in two parts.
>
> 1 **Judgement on James**
>   Look back over this unit so far, and answer the following questions:
>   a What things had James misunderstood about England and the English?
>   b What things had the English misunderstood about James?
>   c When James died in 1625 relations between him and some English people were tense, but it was nowhere near a civil war. Who was to blame for the tension?
>
> Copy and fill in the table below:
>
> | Issues on which James was entirely to blame | Issues on which James was partly to blame | Issues on which James was not to blame at all |
> |---|---|---|
> | | | |
>
> 2 **Advice to Charles**
>   What advice would you give to Charles at the beginning of his reign to help him rule peacefully and successfully? You should include advice on how to handle the three key issues: religion, Parliament, money.

SOURCE 10
Charles I, a painting by Van Dyck from 1635. This painting shows Charles from three different angles.

KINGS AND PARLIAMENTS

SOURCE 11
Henrietta Maria, Charles's French, Roman Catholic wife.

'Our treasures exhausted and our COFFERS empty, we summoned a Parliament, but not finding that success therein which we had just hope to expect, we are resolved to require the aid of our good and loving subjects by lending us a sufficient sum of money to be repaid them as soon as we shall be in any way able to do so.'

SOURCE 12
Charles asking for loans, 1627 (adapted).

Read Source 12 carefully.

1. What reasons does Charles give for asking for these loans?
2. If you received one of these letters from Charles, did you have a choice over whether you lent him money?
3. When would you be paid back?
4. Would *you* have lent the king money in this situation?

After the assassination of Buckingham in 1628, Charles began to rely heavily on his wife, Henrietta Maria (Source 11). This worried many people: she was a princess from France, where kings ruled with complete power. She, and the friends she brought with her from France, were Roman Catholic.

Charles quarrelled with his first Parliament. He needed money to run the country, but Parliament refused to grant him any unless he agreed to their demands. He therefore dismissed Parliament and began to raise money by other means, such as forcing rich people to lend him some (see Source 12).

The Petition of Right

In 1628 war broke out and Charles had to call another Parliament. Parliamentary leaders such as John Pym (Source 13) forced him to sign a document called the Petition of Right. This said he would not collect taxes without their permission or arrest people without trial. To Pym and many MPs, Charles was using his powers in a new way, to set up one-person royal rule. To Charles, Parliament was going beyond anything it had ever done before. He dismissed it in 1629 and began to rule without it.

SOURCE 13
John Pym, Somerset MP, wealthy landowner and merchant. Like many MPs he was a Puritan, educated at university and trained as a lawyer. He first became an MP in 1614 and became a leading critic first of James, then Charles.

KINGS AND PARLIAMENTS

Charles's personal rule 1629 to 1638

If Charles was going to rule without Parliament, he obviously had to cut his costs and raise money. War was his most expensive activity, so he made peace with France and Spain. He used various methods of raising extra money:

- CUSTOMS duties. Parliament normally granted the monarch the right to collect these for life, but the Parliament of 1625 had refused. Charles asked for their collection anyway (see Source 14).
- Forced loans (see Source 12, page 35).
- Monopolies (see page 34).
- Fines. The king had the right to collect fines from law courts. Charles looked into old laws, such as the Forest Laws, and fined people for breaking them.
- Ship money. Coastal counties had sometimes been taxed to provide ships for the navy. In 1634 Charles made this a regular tax and in 1635 extended it to the whole country. This seemed only fair: why shouldn't inland areas pay for the defence of the nation? Many people opposed ship money. A Buckinghamshire gentleman, John Hampden, was sent to prison for refusing to pay (Source 15).

Ship money raised £730,000 between 1634 and 1640. Charles seemed to be able to rule without ever having to call Parliament again. But although he had enough income to rule, he did not have enough for a war.

SOURCE 15
Statue of John Hampden in Aylesbury town centre.

'Finding that it hath continued for many ages and is now an important part of the revenue of the Crown, but could not be settled by Parliament by reason of the dissolution of Parliament, we have therefore ordered that all duties upon goods and MERCHANDISE should be levied in such a manner as were levied in the time of our late dear father King James.'

SOURCE 14
Letter from Charles about customs duties, 1625 (adapted).

Discuss these questions in pairs.

1 Which groups of people would be annoyed by each of Charles's methods of raising money?
2 Who do you feel was behaving unreasonably in the first 13 years of Charles's reign (1625 to 1638): Charles? Parliament? Both? Neither?
3 Do you think governments should tax people?

KINGS AND PARLIAMENTS

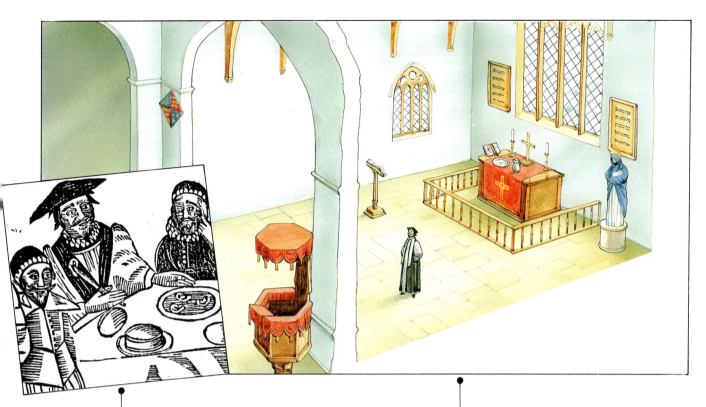

SOURCE 17
A cartoon printed at the time showing Laud eating the ears of William Prynne, a Puritan who had been sentenced to have his ears cut off for criticising Laud's reforms.

SOURCE 16
Church furnished in the way favoured by Charles and Laud.

William Laud

Some people, such as William Laud, believed that the Church of England was too Protestant. They wanted to bring back stained glass windows, a railed-off altar at the east end of the church, more ritual and special clothes for priests (see Source 18). Charles supported this and in 1633 made Laud Archbishop of Canterbury.

The Puritans were very angry at this, but those who protested too much were imprisoned or treated harshly (see Source 17). Then Charles and Laud made a serious mistake: they introduced their ideas into Scotland. If English Puritans were angry, the Scots were furious. The whole country united, thousands signed a National Covenant and formed an army.

Charles called a Parliament and asked for money for an army to crush the Scots. In Parliament John Pym insisted on Charles changing his rule before they would grant a penny. Charles dismissed them, but the Scots invaded England and he had to offer them £850 a day not to move any further south. His policy was in ruins, and he called Parliament again.

> 'This year being Laud's first as Archbishop of Canterbury, great offence was taken when he set up pictures in the windows of his palaces at Lambeth and Croydon, and at his bowing towards the altar which all the people protested against as being POPISH. Mr Ward, a minister in Ipswich preached against bowing at the mention of Jesus' name, for which he was committed to prison, where he lay a long time.'

SOURCE 18
Reactions to Laud's reforms, described by J Rushworth in 1701.

1. Compare Source 16 with the two styles of church in Unit 1: Source 22, page 14 and Source 23, page 15. Do you think the Puritans were right in thinking that Laud was bringing back Roman Catholic ways?
2. Make a list of things Puritans objected to in Laud's reforms.

The drift to civil war

No one wanted a civil war. Charles's attempt to rule on his own was over and he had to do what Parliament wanted. But he was furious with what the Parliamentary leaders were doing, and looked for ways of turning the tables on them.

The first thing Parliament did was to put Laud and the Earl of Strafford in the Tower of London. Strafford had been an MP who changed sides and helped Charles rule. He had been a tough and efficient ruler of the North, then of Ireland. Pym had him put on trial by both Houses of Parliament on a charge of treason (Source 19). The Commons voted by 204 to 59 that he was guilty, the Lords by 26 to 19, and he was executed.

Parliament then set about weakening royal power and strengthening its own. Ship money and forced loans were abolished. Parliament had to meet every three years, and could not be dissolved without its own consent.

By this time many MPs were becoming worried by what Pym was up to. They disliked the continued criticism of the king and the mob violence in the streets of London. They feared that attacks on the king could lead to attacks on the upper classes. Charles went to Scotland and began to gather support there.

Then, with Strafford out of the way, there was a massive rebellion in Ireland. Charles returned to London to ask Parliament for an army to put it down. Parliament feared what Charles might do in England if he had an army and refused. Pym drew up the Grand Remonstrance: a list of all the grievances Parliament had against Charles. It was passed, but the voting was close: 159 to 148.

SOURCE 19
The Trial of the Earl of Strafford, 1641, by both Houses of Parliament. The Lords are on the right, Commons on the left, Strafford is in the centre with his back to us.

The five members

Encouraged by this, Charles came to Parliament with soldiers to arrest Pym and four other leading MPs (see Source 20). They had heard of his plans and escaped down the river into the City of London. Charles's action seemed to prove that he could not be trusted.

Charles moved out of London and began to look for support. In August 1642 he raised his flag at Nottingham and called on all loyal subjects of military age to join him. Some, like Edward Hyde (see Source 22) were convinced he was in the right; others, like Sir Edmund Verney, were not at all convinced, but fought for him out of sheer old-fashioned loyalty to the Crown. Parliament also prepared for war. Among those who took up arms for Parliament was Sir Edmund's son, Sir Ralph Verney. The Civil War had begun.

'The King came for those five gentlemen. Then he called Mr Pym by name, and no answer was made. Then he asked the Speaker if they were there or where they were.

Upon that the Speaker fell on his knees and said that he was a servant of the House and neither had eyes nor tongue to hear or say anything but what Parliament commanded. Then the King told him he thought that his eyes were as good as his, and then said his birds had flown but he did expect the House would send them to him. He assured us they would have a fair trial, and so went out.'

SOURCE 20
Extract from a letter written by Sir Ralph Verney, describing Charles's attempt to arrest the five MPs, January 1642.

SOURCE 21
17th-century print of Charles raising his standard (flag) at Nottingham, August 1642.

'You have the satisfaction of believing you are in the right, that the King ought not to grant what is required of him. But for my part I do not like the quarrel and wish the King would consent to what they desire. My only concern now is to follow my master. I have served him for 30 years and will not do so base a thing as to desert him now.'

SOURCE 22
Sir Edmund Verney's words just before his death at the battle of Edgehill, October 1642, recorded by his friend Edward Hyde. Sir Edmund Verney was Sir Ralph's father.

attainment target

1. Give one reason why some people chose to fight for:
   a the king and
   b Parliament.

2. Divide your page into three columns with the headings shown. Fill in as many causes under each heading as you can.

Causes which go back before 1629	Causes which go back before 1640	Causes which emerged after 1640

3. For each cause you have chosen write the letter P, R, S or E against it, to say whether you think it was:
   Political (P) – to do with the actions of kings or Parliament
   Religious (R) – to do with the Church and styles of worship
   Economic (E) – to do with money and trade
   Social (S) – to do with different types of people in society.

4. Are any of these types of cause linked together? Explain one such link.

5. Which type of cause (political, religious, economic or social) do you think was the most important? Explain your answer.

The division of England

The arguments between king and Parliament split the country (Source 24). They even split families, and old friends found themselves fighting one another (see Source 25). Many people, however, had nothing to do with the fighting. The marching armies and their demands for food disrupted trade and farming. In Dorset and Somerset the 'Clubmen' took up arms against both sides to keep them out of their areas.

The king's support came from the more traditional areas and the old nobility. Many of these were skilled horsemen and used to weapons. They were called 'cavaliers', which means horsemen. The king's nephew, Prince Rupert, led the Royalist cavalry with great success in early battles.

Parliament's supporters came mainly from lesser gentry, townspeople and merchants (see Source 26). The backing of apprentice boys who had short hair gave them their nickname of 'roundheads'. But Parliament had three great advantages which would help it in the long run:
- South-East England was richer, and so could pay for a long war.
- The Navy supported Parliament, so it was difficult for the king to get men and supplies from abroad.
- Before he died in December 1642, Pym set up a well-organised system to supply Parliament's army with money.

SOURCE 23
The equipment of a Civil War cavalry soldier.

SOURCE 24
How the country divided in the Civil War.

SOURCE 25
'The experience I have had of your worth and the happiness I have enjoyed in your friendship are wounding considerations when I look at this present distance between us. My affection for you is unchangeable, but I must be true to the cause in which I serve. The great God knows with what a sad sense I go upon this service and with what a perfect hatred I detest this war without an enemy. Your most affectionate friend, and faithful servant, William Waller.'

Extract from a letter from William Waller to Ralph Hopton, 1643 (adapted). The men were old friends. William Waller was a general on Parliament's side; Ralph Hopton was a Royalist general.

SOURCE 26
'A people of inferior degree who by good farming, the cloth trade and other thriving businesses had gotten very good fortunes, were fast friends to Parliament.'

This sentence describing Somerset is from *The History of the Great Rebellion*, by the royalist Edward Hyde, Lord Clarendon.

The New Model Army

We read in Source 22 that Sir Edmund Verney took up arms reluctantly. The same was true on Parliament's side: some people were unsure if they should defeat their king in battle. This was no way to fight a war.

Oliver Cromwell, the MP for Cambridge, began to show his skill as cavalry commander of the parliamentary army from East Anglia. He promoted people for their ability, not for how important they were (see Source 27). He allowed Puritans of all kinds to worship in whatever way they wanted. He himself believed that God was on his side, and saw proof of this in his victories (see Source 28). In return he expected loyalty, good discipline and strict training from his men.

In 1644 Parliament set up the New Model Army. This defeated the king at Marston Moor in 1644 and at Naseby in 1645 (Source 29). At Naseby it was Cromwell's disciplined cavalry, halting their charge and attacking the Royalist infantry, which turned the battle. By then the Scots had joined in on Parliament's side and the king was facing defeat. He surrendered to the Scots in 1646 and they handed him over to the English. Charles talked terms with the Army, but in 1647 he escaped and made a deal with the Scots. Cromwell defeated the Scots and Royalists at the battle of Preston in 1648.

> Give me a russet-coated captain that knows what he fights for and loves what he knows than that which you call a gentleman and is nothing else.

SOURCE 27
Oliver Cromwell describes his attitude to promotion in the New Model Army.

> I could not, riding about my business, but smile out to God in praises, in assurance of victory.

SOURCE 28
Cromwell, speaking before the battle of Naseby.

SOURCE 29
The forces before the battle of Naseby, 1645. The Royalist army is at the top, with the king in front of it. Prince Rupert's cavalry is on the Royalist right. The Parliamentary Army is at the bottom, commanded by Sir Thomas Fairfax. Oliver Cromwell is on the right.

UNIT 4

Searching for a settlement

AIMS

In this unit we will see that putting the king on trial and executing him posed all kinds of problems. Over the years 1649 to 1714 many people tried to find a government which had both the right and the power to rule. There were short periods when things seemed to be working out, but they soon went wrong again. We will learn about some of these ideas for government in this unit.

We will also find out how these dramatic events in England had important effects on Scotland and Ireland. You will see why this book is called *The Making of the United Kingdom*.

We saw at the end of unit 3 that some people on Parliament's side were not sure about fighting against their king. We also saw that Cromwell and the New Model Army had no such doubts. They thought that Charles had been untrustworthy and unreasonable. They blamed him for the war and called him 'the man of blood'. They feared that as long as he was alive another outbreak of civil war was always possible.

Cromwell put Charles on trial. Even then many feared the worst. The Parliamentary general, Fairfax, failed to appear at the trial. The court president, John Bradshaw, wore a reinforced hat in case he was attacked (Source 4).

SOURCE 1
Painting of the execution of Charles, January 1649. The four small pictures show: top left, Charles; bottom left, Charles walking to his execution; top right, the executioner holding up Charles's head; bottom right, people dipping their handkerchiefs in his blood.

The king's execution

The charges against Charles were that he had tried to rule on his own and ignore the laws. He was charged with treason and complete responsibility for the war (see Source 2).

Charles refused to accept that the court had any right to try him. He pointed out that he was the rightful king and so could not be accused of treason, which means attacking the king (see Source 3).

There was never any doubt about the court's verdict. Charles was found guilty and his death warrant signed by 59 of his 135 judges. He was executed on 30 January 1649. As the poet Andrew Marvell wrote:

'He nothing common did or mean
Upon that memorable scene.'

His execution was greeted by the crowd not with a cheer but with a groan. Several people soaked their handkerchiefs in his blood. These bloody handkerchiefs were later said to have caused miraculous cures from illnesses. Royalism was obviously not dead.

The country now had to face two serious questions:
- Who had the right to rule?
- Who had the power to rule?

The next 65 years were to see several different answers to both these questions.

'Charles Stuart, King of England, trusted to govern according to the laws of the land, had a wicked design to create for himself an unlimited power to rule according to his will and to overthrow the rights and liberties of the people. To do this he treacherously waged a war against Parliament and the people. He is thus responsible for all the treasons, murders, rapings, burnings, damage and desolation caused during the wars. He is therefore a TYRANT, traitor and murderer.'

SOURCE 2
The charge against King Charles at his trial in January 1649.

I wish to know by what power I am brought here – I would know by what lawful authority. Remember I am your king, your lawful king . . . I say think well upon it . . . I have a trust committed to me by God, by old and lawful descent. I will not betray it to a new and unlawful authority.

SOURCE 3
Charles's criticism of the court which was putting him on trial, 1649.

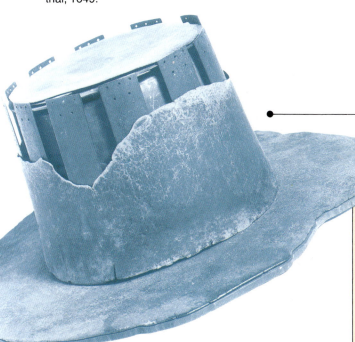

SOURCE 4
Metal hat worn by John Bradshaw, president of the court.

Discuss these questions in your groups.

1 Do you agree that Charles was
  a 'a man of blood', guilty of treason (Source 2), or
  b a king who could not be put on trial (Source 3)?

2 135 MPs and army officers were appointed as judges. Many did not turn up; 70 declared him guilty and only 59 signed Charles's death warrant. Why do you think this was?

3 Why did the execution of Charles pose problems for the country?

SEARCHING FOR A SETTLEMENT

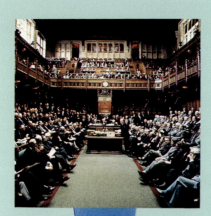
The House of Commons

Saddam Hussein ruler of Iraq, 1991

The French Revolution, 1789

THE RIGHT TO RULE
Parliament, MPs, have the RIGHT TO RULE because they have been chosen by the people in an election.

THE POWER TO RULE
In some countries the army has taken over without an election. They have the POWER TO RULE by force as no one can stop them.

REVOLUTION
In a revolution old ideas of who has the right to rule are thrown out as the people seize power for themselves.

England without a king 1649 to 1660

As you can see from the diagram above the people who have the power to rule are not always the same as the people who have the right to rule. In England in 1649, the victorious Army had the power, but Parliament claimed the right because it had been elected. The leader of the army, Oliver Cromwell (Source 5), made several attempts to bring the two together over the next few years.

The world turned upside down

To some people the Civil War had turned the world upside down. Until then, ordinary people had no power (see Source 6). Now some of them had joined an army which had dared to fight against and defeat the king. Ideas for changing the law, the Church and the system of voting were discussed. Thousands of PAMPHLETS were printed.

SOURCE 6
From Sir Thomas Smith's *Description of England*, 1565 (adapted).

SOURCE 5
Oliver Cromwell in 1656

'Day labourers, shopkeepers which have no land of their own, smallholders and craftsmen have no voice in our Commonwealth and no account is made of them but to be ruled.'

Among the groups that wanted to make an English Revolution were:

- The Levellers. These people wanted most adult men to have a vote. They had a strong following in the Army and debates were held between Army leaders and the Levellers at Putney in 1647.
- The Diggers. These people wanted the right to all common land (see Source 7). They set up communes, farming land at St George's Hill, Cobham.

These ideas really did turn the world of the 17th century upside down. Cromwell did not support either of them, and the groups were crushed by force.

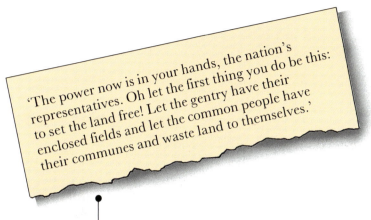

SOURCE 7
Extract from a pamphlet written by Gerard Winstanley appealing to Parliament, 1649. Winstanley was the leader of the Diggers.

'The power now is in your hands, the nation's representatives. Oh let the first thing you do be this: to set the land free! Let the gentry have their enclosed fields and let the common people have their communes and waste land to themselves.'

Cromwell's search for a settlement

The Rump Parliament 1649 to 1653
Of all the MPs who had been elected in 1640, less than half were left, and all those who supported the king were removed. Cromwell realised the Rump had no real right to rule, and dismissed it in 1653.

The Barebones Parliament 1653 to 1654
Cromwell and the Army now chose 140 MPs whom they trusted. These included a London leather-seller called Praise-God Barebones. However, they talked too much and did nothing, so Cromwell dismissed them.

The Major-Generals 1654 to 1657
Cromwell now became Lord Protector and ruled with one of his major-generals in charge of each region. This was highly unpopular. These men had no right to rule, just the power of the Army behind them.

Restoration 1660
To many people it seemed as if the only person with a right to rule was a king. Cromwell was offered the Crown, but after much hesitation, refused it. He died in 1658. His son Richard could not command the respect his father had, and resigned in 1659. There was confusion for nearly a year until General Monck and his army marched to London, took control and invited Charles I's son to come back as King Charles II.

ACTIVITY

Get into groups of four. You are all from Parliament's side:

1. A Puritan soldier in the New Model Army. You have had friends killed by Charles's soldiers in battle. You trust Oliver Cromwell who seems to promote people on their merits, and you support the Levellers.
2. A rich merchant who opposed the King in 1640, but felt that Parliament had gone too far by 1642. You are worried by the power of the Army and the ideas of people like the soldier, Number 1.
3. A landowner who supported Parliament in the Civil War, but felt it was wrong to execute the king.
4. A shopkeeper who finds that the disruption caused by the Civil War makes business difficult.

You must discuss among yourselves to reach a decision on who should rule England, and how. The discussion takes place:
a in 1649, after the death of Charles,
b in 1658, after the death of Oliver Cromwell.

SEARCHING FOR A SETTLEMENT

SOURCE 8
The coronation procession of King Charles II.

The return of the monarchy

To all Royalists, and to many who weren't, by 1660 the only answer to the question 'who had the right to rule?' was King Charles II. He was given a tremendous welcome on his return to England and a splendid coronation (see Source 8). Parliament granted him an income of £1,200,000, far more than Charles I had managed on in the 1630s. He seemed therefore to have the power, as well as the right, to rule.

Real power after 1660, however, lay with the rich landowners who now controlled Parliament. They had been horrified by the democratic ideas and freedom of worship of the 1640s and 1650s. They were resentful of the people of lower social class who had ruled the country in those years. They hated the very name of Oliver Cromwell, and had his dead body dug up and hanged. Those people still alive in England who had signed Charles I's death warrant were arrested and executed. The old prayer book was restored and 1,760 ministers who refused to accept it were removed from the Church of England. In 1664 religious worship outside the Church of England was banned. Members of Puritan groups, such as the Quakers, who had flourished under Oliver Cromwell, were fined and imprisoned.

Parliament believed in the monarchy, and thought the upheavals were over. But no one could wipe away history: Charles I had been opposed, defeated and executed; Charles II had been invited to become king. MPs might not have agreed with the idea, but a king could clearly be un-made as well as made. By 1688 MPs had to face this, because the king was doing the one thing which turned the country against him.

SOURCE 9
King James II.

James II

We have already seen that by the 17th century most people were violently anti-Roman Catholic. Some idea of the strength of feeling can be seen in Source 10. Charles II died in 1685, becoming a Roman Catholic on his deathbed. His brother James (Source 9), who became James II, was already a Roman Catholic.

The laws said that only members of the Church of England could hold important jobs. Kings could remove laws in certain cases and James began to do this to put Roman Catholics into the army, universities and local government. He also got his supporters elected to Parliament (Source 11).

James's heir was his daughter Mary, who was Protestant and married to his Protestant nephew William of Orange. Many people were worried and angry about James's Roman Catholic views, but felt the future was safe. Then his new Roman Catholic wife gave birth to a son. Secret contacts had been made with William and in November 1688 he arrived in England (Source 12). As he slowly made his way from Devon to London, James's supporters slipped away to join him. James fled to France and William and Mary became joint monarchs as William III and Mary II.

> Having been called by Almighty God to rule these kingdoms, I think of nothing but the spread of the Catholic religion. This is the true service of God for which I am willing to sacrifice everything.

SOURCE 11
James II's religious views.

> 'Imagine you see troops of Papists ravishing your wives and daughters and plundering your houses. Casting your eye towards Smithfield imagine you see your father or your mother or some of your nearest and dearest relations tied to a stake in the midst of flames – this was a frequent spectacle the last time Papacy reigned among us.'

SOURCE 10
Extract from an anti-Roman Catholic pamphlet of 1679.

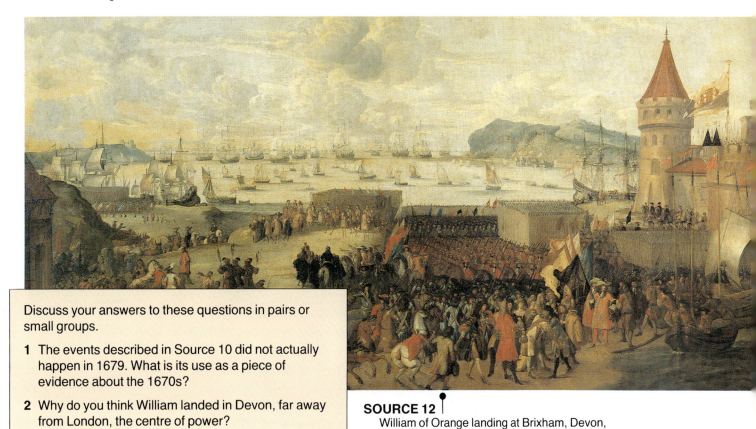

SOURCE 12
William of Orange landing at Brixham, Devon, 5 November 1688.

Discuss your answers to these questions in pairs or small groups.

1 The events described in Source 10 did not actually happen in 1679. What is its use as a piece of evidence about the 1670s?

2 Why do you think William landed in Devon, far away from London, the centre of power?

SEARCHING FOR A SETTLEMENT

The Glorious Revolution

The extraordinary events of 1688 and 1689 have been called the 'Bloodless Revolution' or the 'Glorious Revolution'. Are these good names for what happened?

The take-over of the throne by William and Mary was bloodless in England, Wales but not in Scotland, or, as we shall see, in Ireland. It was only a revolution at the top. The monarch changed, but there was no change in the people who held power (see Source 13). These were the rich landowners who controlled Parliament. There was no change in this situation for 150 years. For them it was indeed a 'Glorious Revolution'.

The Settlement

In 1689, and over the next few years, relations between monarchs and Parliament were settled, leaving monarchs in much the same position as they hold now.

- No monarch could be a Roman Catholic.
- Only Parliament could pass laws and monarchs could not dispense with them as James II had done.
- People were allowed to worship freely. This excluded Roman Catholics and all university and government jobs were still reserved for members of the Church of England. Nevertheless, Quakers and other groups were able to build chapels or meeting houses of their own (see Source 14).
- Parliamentary elections had to be held at least every three years.

'For both the Protestant religion and the laws and liberties of the nation. Our expectation is intended for no other design but to have a free and lawful Parliament assembled as soon as possible.'

SOURCE 13
From William's Declaration of why he had landed in England, 1688.

William brought England into the war against France he had been fighting since 1686. The war was almost permanent, going on from 1689 to 1697 and 1702 to 1713. This was very expensive: the army alone cost £2.7 million a year. William could not keep asking Parliament for money, so they came to an arrangement:

- Parliament would take over the cost of the army, raising money from taxes.
- Parliament had the right to decide foreign policy.
- The monarch was given an income from the Civil List.

SOURCE 14
Long Sutton Quaker meeting house, Somerset, built in 1707.

SEARCHING FOR A SETTLEMENT

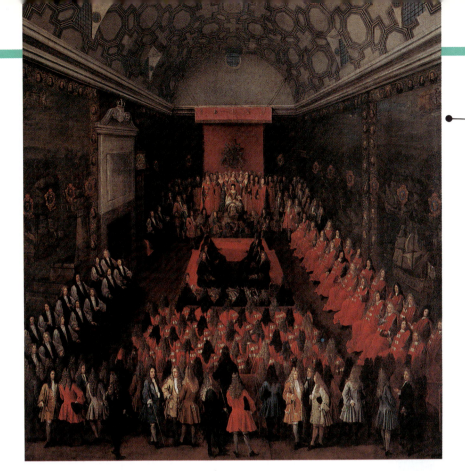

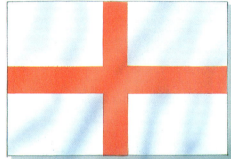

SOURCE 15
Queen Anne in the House of Lords.

SOURCE 16
The Union Flag, formed from the flags of England, Scotland and Ireland.

The Act of Union 1707

William and Mary had no children. Their successor, Mary's sister Anne, had 17 babies, all of whom died young. The English Parliament looked to the rulers of Hanover in Germany, descendants of James I, to become monarchs after Anne (see family tree on page 4). Scotland, however, was still a separate country. Oliver Cromwell had united the two for a brief period (1652 to 1660) after he had defeated the Scots. Now the Scots demanded the right to choose their own ruler. Many Scots were loyal to the Stuarts, and wanted James II's son to rule. This could bring Scotland into the wars on France's side.

This was unthinkable to the English, so an Act of Union was passed in 1707 on terms which the Scots could agree. 45 Scottish MPs and 16 Scottish peers entered Parliament. They kept their own Church, law and education but could trade on the same terms as English merchants. The United Kingdom of England, Scotland, Ireland and Wales was formed.

attainment target

These questions are about people's attitudes and motives during the events described in these pages.

1 Why did so many people leave James and join William as he made his way from Brixham to London?

2 Why did William make the promises in Source 13?

3 Many people after 1660 thought that monarchs should always be obeyed completely. How would they react to the events of 1688?

4 Why did Parliament want regular elections?

5 Why did William and Mary accept all the limitations on their power listed opposite?

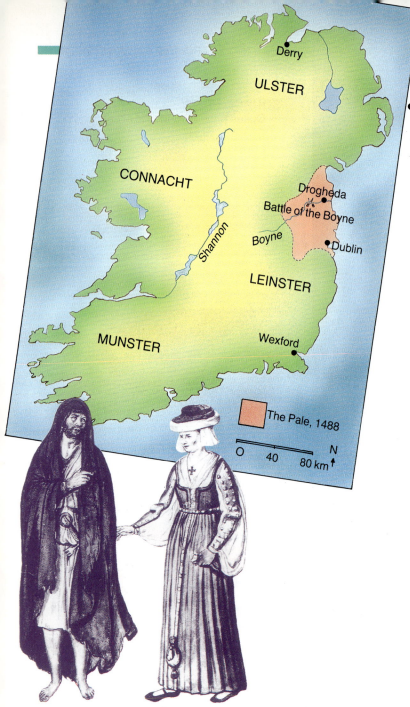

SOURCE 17
Map of Ireland.

SOURCE 18
An illustration of 1575 showing a woman from the Pale and a Gaelic Irishman.

> An old woman, which was his foster-mother, took up his head when he was quartered, and sucked up all the blood running thereout, saying that the earth was not worthy to drink it.

SOURCE 19
The poet Edmund Spenser, secretary to Queen Elizabeth's representative in Ireland, describes the execution of Murrough O'Brien in 1583. O'Brien was hanged, drawn and quartered by the English. That is he was first hanged, and while still alive, his insides were cut out and then his body cut into four parts.

Ireland in 1500

English monarchs had called themselves Kings of Ireland ever since 1155. However, the only part of Ireland which they really controlled at the end of the Middle Ages was an area around Dublin called 'the Pale' (see Source 17). 'Beyond the Pale' lords and chiefs ruled like little kings. Some of these lords were descended from Norman barons who had taken land in Ireland in the 12th century. Others, like the rest of the people, were Gaelic, with their own language, poetry, laws and customs. Warfare between the chiefs was common. This made a settled farming life very difficult for ordinary people. They grew some crops, but mostly kept huge herds of cattle, which grazed on the move over a wide area.

A vicious circle

The English did not understand the Irish: because they were different, the English regarded them as uncivilised. This can be seen in Source 18, where the Irishman is shown as a wild savage. In Source 19, Spenser obviously thought the old woman's action was barbaric, but that hanging, drawing and quartering was not.

Religion helped to turn this mistrust into hatred. When England became Protestant, Ireland stayed firmly Roman Catholic. The Bible and Prayer Book in English meant nothing to the Gaelic-speaking people. In Queen Elizabeth's reign, the Pope told the Irish that they did not have to obey their English rulers. Irish rebellions now posed a new danger to England in their war with Catholic Spain. Spanish forces helped the rebels and so might gain a base close to England. There were four Irish rebellions in Elizabeth's reign, and her government had to send large armies to put them down. Many Irish were killed.

Plantations

The English came up with a solution to their Irish 'problem'. The Irish people, they thought, were uncivilised, Roman Catholic rebels, so should be replaced by civilised, Protestant English settlers. Land was taken from the Irish and handed out to English or Scottish farming families as 'plantations'. About ten settler families were 'planted' on each 1,000 acres (see Source 21). These settlers introduced English farming methods, sold off the cattle, and grew crops. The Irish were employed as labourers on the land they had once used themselves. In 1603, Roman Catholics owned 90% of Ireland. By 1641 they owned only 59%.

So a vicious circle of hatred grew up (see Source 20). There was brutality on both sides. English settlers would only go to Ireland if they felt safe, so Irish opposition was harshly crushed. When the Irish did rise up in protest in 1641, they attacked English settlers and 2,000 were MASSACRED (see Source 22).

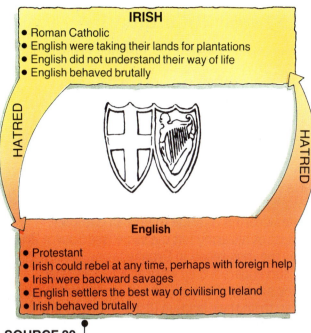

SOURCE 20
The 'vicious circle'.

SOURCE 21
The Vintners' Settlement at Bellaghy, Ulster, 1622.

SOURCE 22
A Protestant view of the Irish rebels of 1641.

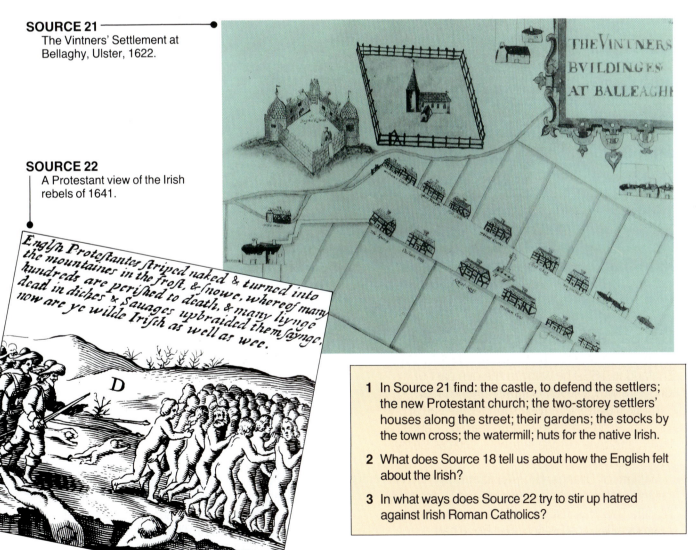

1. In Source 21 find: the castle, to defend the settlers; the new Protestant church; the two-storey settlers' houses along the street; their gardens; the stocks by the town cross; the watermill; huts for the native Irish.

2. What does Source 18 tell us about how the English felt about the Irish?

3. In what ways does Source 22 try to stir up hatred against Irish Roman Catholics?

Cromwell and Ireland

Pictures such as Source 22 horrified Protestants in England. As soon as the Civil War was won, Oliver Cromwell went to Ireland. He wanted revenge for the massacres of 1641, and permanent peace for Ireland. For him, permanent peace meant expelling all priests and rebels, taking most of the land away from Roman Catholics, and trying to convert the Irish to Protestantism. As we have seen (see page 41), Cromwell was tolerant towards different Protestant views, but Source 23 makes clear his attitude to Roman Catholics.

Most of his army felt the same (see Source 24). After the Irish rebels in Drogheda and Wexford had surrendered, they were all killed and the towns SACKED. Roman Catholic landowners were driven from their lands in Ulster, Munster and Leinster and bundled on to poor land west of the River Shannon. Thousands of acres of land were given to Protestant settlers. A strip of land, four miles wide, along the River Shannon, was given to Protestant soldier-settlers. By 1665, only 22% of Ireland was in Roman Catholic hands, mostly in Connacht.

But Cromwell's plans to convert the Irish to Protestantism failed. Ireland therefore now had Protestant, English-speaking landowners dominating Roman Catholic, Gaelic-speaking peasants.

> I meddle not with any man's conscience, but if by liberty of conscience you mean a liberty to exercise the Mass [the Roman Catholic service] I judge it best to use plain dealing and to let you know . . . that will not be allowed of.

SOURCE 23
In 1650 Oliver Cromwell was asked by an Irish Roman Catholic that people should be allowed to worship according to their own beliefs (their conscience). This was his reply.

SOURCE 24
St George, dressed as a Cromwellian soldier, trampling on the Irish dragon, 1649.

The battle of the Boyne, July 1690

When the Roman Catholic James II fled from England in 1689 he went to the one part of his kingdom which would support him: Roman Catholic Ireland. The Irish soon formed an army for him. Protestants in Ireland feared a repeat of 1641, and took refuge in towns, such as Derry, which were beseiged.

William of Orange, King William III, arrived in Ireland with a combined English and Dutch army. To him, this was just part of his long war with James's allies, the French. The Pope had quarrelled with the French and in fact supported William. His forces defeated James at the battle of the Boyne in July 1690 (see Source 25). The Irish went on to fight other battles, but peace was made in 1691.

The Protestant victory

After William's victory the Protestants in Ireland made sure their control was complete. Roman Catholics were banned from Parliament, the law, university and the navy. They could not vote, run a

SEARCHING FOR A SETTLEMENT

SOURCE 25
A contemporary picture of King William III at the battle of the Boyne. William is on horseback at the centre of the group of horsemen in the bottom right-hand corner.

SOURCE 26
'King Billy', a modern painting on a wall in Belfast.

school, or own a horse worth more than £5. Roman Catholic bishops were BANISHED and could be hanged, drawn and quartered if they returned. Only a few registered priests were allowed. Roman Catholics found it difficult to inherit land and the amount they had fell to 14% by 1703, 5% by 1776.

The battle of the Boyne was thus very important to Protestants. To this day pictures of 'King Billy' can be seen on walls and banners in Protestant parts of Northern Ireland (Source 26).

attainment target

1 'In the 17th century the English treated the Irish badly.' Is this statement a fact or a point of view?

2 What do you think about the way the English ruled in Ireland in this period? Which out of Sources 17 to 26 would you use to support your interpretation?

3 Compare Source 25 and 26. The Ulster Protestant who painted Source 26 saw William as a Protestant hero protecting Ireland from the Pope and Roman Catholics. What facts does this view of William seem to ignore?

4 Why do you think the battle of the Boyne is seen as such an important event in Irish history?

UNIT 5

Restoration London

Samuel Pepys (Source 1) was born in 1633. He had a successful career as a government official in charge of the Navy under Charles II and James II. His fame today, however, comes from the detailed diary he kept from 1660 until he gave it up because of bad eyesight in 1669.

Pepys was a Londoner, and his diary tells us as much about London as about him. The entry for 16 January 1660 in Source 2, for example, tells us about his love of music and friendship and about London's 'bellmen' or nightwatchmen. At that time London had many old buildings, dating back to the 16th century and earlier, crowded around the narrow streets, the river and the one bridge (Source 3). It was quicker to go by boat on the river than along the narrow streets. There were new habits in London, too, such as the coffee houses (Source 4). Coffee was a new drink and by 1663 there were 82 coffee houses in London. Here Pepys and his friends could have lively discussions.

AIMS

In this unit we will find out about Pepys's London, and the similarities and differences between it and London of our own day. London in Pepys's time had a mixture of old and new buildings. We will also discover that people at this time had a mixture of old and new ideas, attitudes and beliefs as well.

> To the Green Dragon on Lambeth Hill. We sang all sorts of things and I played my FLAGEOLET. Stayed there until 9 o'clock, very merry and drawn on with one song after another till it came to be so late. After that we went to Westminster on foot and at the Golden Lion at Charing Cross we went in and drank a pint of wine and so parted. Thence home. I sat up till the bellman came by, just under my window as I was writing of this very line, and cried 'Past one o'clock on a cold frosty windy morning.'

SOURCE 2
From Pepys's *Diary* for 16 January 1660.

SOURCE 1
Samuel Pepys in 1666, aged 33.

SOURCE 3
London Bridge and the River Thames.

Sometimes Pepys's diary highlights the differences between his world and ours, as in his menu for a dinner for six (Source 5). This is also clear when he records important national events, such as the Great Plague of 1665 in which 100,000 Londoners died (Source 6).

'At noon came my guests. I had a pretty dinner for them: a brace of stewed carp, six roasted chickens, and a salmon, hot, for the first course and a tansy [egg pudding flavoured with tansy flowers], two ox-tongues and cheese, the second.'

SOURCE 5
From Pepys's *Diary* for 26 March 1662.

June 7 I did in Drury Lane see two or three houses marked with a red cross upon the door and 'Lord have mercy upon us' writ there, which was a sad sight to me. I was forced to buy some roll-tobacco to smell and to chew.

August 12 The people die so that now it seems they have to carry their dead to be buried by daylight, the nights not being long enough to do it in.

SOURCE 6
Entries from Pepys's *Diary* for 1665.

SOURCE 4
A London coffee house. Coffee pots are being kept warm by the fire. On the left a waiter is collecting long clay pipes for customers.

1. In what ways does Samuel Pepys's menu of 26 March 1662 differ from a meal for guests in your own home today?
2. What do these sources tell us about the personality of Samuel Pepys?
3. The differences between London life in the 1660s and today are very clear, but what similarities can you find in these sources between then and now?

RESTORATION LONDON

Pepys's London

By the 1660s probably 25% of the population of England lived in towns. This was much more than a 100 years earlier. London had by far the biggest population: perhaps ½ million people in Pepys's day. London was the centre of trade, business, banking, publishing, government, entertainment, fashion – and crime. The theatres, which had been closed down under the Protectorate, reopened with great success after Charles II's return in 1660 (Source 7). All these people flocking to London caused terrible overcrowding and new buildings sprawled into the countryside (see Source 8).

The Great Fire

The Great Fire of 1666 (see Sources 9 and 10) destroyed 13,200 houses and 87 churches, as well as shops and warehouses. One reason for the rapid spread of the fire was the fact that London was a city built of timber, bone dry after a hot summer. Another reason was that although pumps like the one in Source 11 had been invented, most were destroyed at the beginning of the fire. Pulling down houses seemed the only way to stop the fire spreading.

> Mr Sheply and I to the new playhouse near Lincoln's Inn Fields (which was formerly Gibbons' tennis court) where the play of *Beggar's Bush* was newly begun. It was well acted, and here I saw the first time one Moore, who is said to be the best actor in the world, lately come over with the King. And indeed it is the finest playhouse, I believe, that ever was in England.

SOURCE 7
From Pepys's *Diary* for 20 November 1660.

> 'On Mayday in the morning every man would walk in the sweet meadows and green woods, but now the countryside is much pestered with building.'

SOURCE 8
From John Stow's description of London in 1600.

SOURCE 9
The Great Fire of London, September 1666. The fire started in a baker's shop in Pudding Lane on 1 September. This painting shows the scene on the night of 3 September. Old St Paul's can be seen burning in the centre of the picture.

RESTORATION LONDON

'So I down to the waterside and there got a boat and saw a lamentable fire. Everybody endeavouring to remove their goods and flinging them into the river or bringing them into boats. Poor people staying in their houses until the fire touched them, and then running into boats. The poor pigeons were loath to leave their houses, but hovered about the balconies till they were some of them burnt and fell down.

[Pepys went to the king, who told him to tell the Lord Mayor to pull down all the houses in the fire's path. Pepys then went to watch the fire again]

... We to a little alehouse on the Bankside and there stayed till it was dark and saw the fire grow, more and more, in corners and upon steeples and between churches and houses as far as we could see up the hill of the City in a most horrid, malicious, bloody flame. It made me weep to see it. The churches, houses, all on fire and flaming at once and a horrid noise the flames made, and the cracking of houses at their ruin.'

SOURCE 10
From Pepys's *Diary* for 2 September 1666.

SOURCE 11
A 17th-century water-pump for fire-fighting.

The new London

Pepys died in 1703, by which time London had a very different skyline. Among the most prominent buildings in Source 12 are the new St Paul's, begun in 1670 and designed by Sir Christopher Wren, and some of the 15 other churches he designed.

SOURCE 12
View of London in 1751.

attainment target

1 Samuel Pepys lived in London almost continuously from 1646 until his death. What differences would he have found between the London he knew as a youth and the London of his old age?

2 'London: the most exciting place in Britain in the 1660s.' Choose four sources from pages 54 to 57 which show that you agree or disagree with this statement. Explain why you have chosen each one.

3 Explain how your four sources show agreement or disagreement with the statement.

Old and new ideas

There were not just old and new buildings and fashions in Pepys's time, but old and new ideas too. We have seen throughout this book that religion was a powerful force in people's lives. To some, a strong belief in God meant a belief in the Devil too. That also meant believing in witches. Such people believed that witches were women (and some men) who had become the Devil's servants. Women were tried and hanged for witchcraft (see Source 13). James I was a great believer in witches.

In 1644 Matthew Hopkins set himself up as Witchfinder-General, travelling about East Anglia charging a fee for the discovery of witches. Suspected women were stripped, tied cross-legged on a table and kept without food or sleep until they confessed. They were then hanged. In 1661 Sir Matthew Hale, one of Charles II's judges, tried two women for causing children to faint and vomit pins and nails. They were both found guilty of witchcraft and executed.

The scientific revolution

Scientists approach problems by observing, measuring and recording things that happen. Throughout Europe in the 17th century scientists were producing scientific explanations based on their observations, and not on what they were told to believe, or on magic.

Sometimes this got them into trouble with the Church. Galileo, an Italian astronomer, was arrested in 1632 for challenging the Church's teaching that the Sun and planets moved round the Earth.

Charles II, unlike his grandfather, did not believe in witches. He was curious about many things and interested in science. In 1662 a group of scientists founded a society to meet and discuss their ideas. Charles agreed to become its president, and the Royal Society is still a leading scientific society today. One early member was the Earl of Orrery, who was interested in the movement of the Sun, Moon and planets (Source 14).

SOURCE 13
Three women hanged as witches at Chelmsford, Essex in 1589. The weird little animals were the witches' 'familiars' or devilish creatures who carried out their instructions.

SOURCE 14
Early 18th century model of the solar system called an orrery. The Sun is at the centre, with the orbits of the planets in rings around it.

SOURCE 15
Illustration from William Harvey's book, published in 1628, on the circulation of the blood. In the top drawing he shows that if a tight bandage is put on the arm, the valves show up on the swollen vein (B, C, D, E). In the lower drawing, if a finger is pressed along the vein from O to H the vein empties and does not refill. The valve at O must be a one-way valve, only permitting the blood to move towards the heart. The vein only refills if the finger is removed from it.

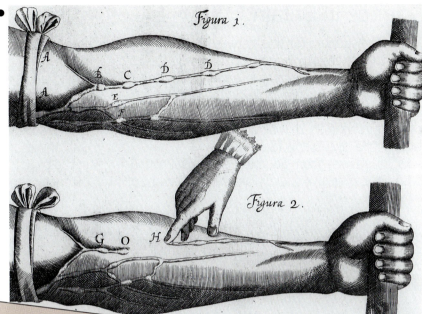

'It is proved that blood is transferred through the lungs to the heart as in a water-pump. It is proved that there is a transit of blood from the arteries to the veins and from this it is shown that the perpetual movement of the blood in a circle is brought about by the heart.'

SOURCE 16
From William Harvey's book.

SOURCE 17
From an account of the death of Charles II written by one of his doctors.

William Harvey

William Harvey was an English doctor, who lived from 1578 to 1657. He wanted to make a career in medicine, so he went to study at the great medical school at Padua in Italy. Here lecturers dissected human bodies to explain how they worked. For centuries people had believed that blood moved from the heart out to all parts of the body, where it was used up just as logs are burnt in a fire. If you were ill it could be that you had too much blood, so doctors would 'bleed' patients deliberately.

Harvey approached this problem scientifically. He measured the amount of blood passing out of the heart in an hour. It came to about three times the weight of an adult! Obviously this amount of blood could not be made every hour. The answer must be that the blood circulates, with the heart acting as a pump (see Sources 11, 15 and 16).

Source 17 shows how far medicine still had to go before treatments became more scientific and less like magic. It was many years before Harvey's discovery had any effect on medical treatments.

> **February 2nd, 1685.** His Majesty King Charles II, having just left his bed was walking quietly when he felt some unusual disturbance in his brain, soon followed by a loss of speech and CONVULSIONS. There happened to be present at the time two of the King's Physicians. They opened a vein in his right arm and drew off 16 ounces of blood.
> **February 4th.** The Physicians considered it advisable to administer the following small draught: Spirit of Human Skull, 40 drops in an ounce and a half of Cordial.
> **February 6th.** 1½ drams of Peruvian Bark in 3 ounces of wine, to be mixed and taken at once. The King died the same day, aged 54.

1. What would a modern scientist think about the activities of Matthew Hopkins, self-styled 'Witchfinder-General'?
2. What would a modern scientist think about the treatments given to the dying Charles II (Source 17)?

RESTORATION LONDON

Science in Britain

Charles II's support for science was important. It meant that scientists were not attacked by the Church for undermining their teaching. Charles also made science fashionable: Samuel Pepys was attracted to join, even though he had the honesty to admit in his diary that he didn't understand some of the discussions (Source 20).

As you can see from Sources 19 and 20, trying to find out, measure and explain the movement of Sun and stars interested everybody. Comets were particularly interesting as they used to be regarded as mysterious signs of bad luck. Old theories of the solar system could not explain them, but Robert Hooke's 'new opinion' (Source 20) was close to the truth.

Many people, including Charles, were interested in the practical uses of science, Source 18, for example, shows his concern for the navy, for

SOURCE 18
Charles II as President of the Royal Society. Charles points to a telescope; the picture also includes two globes, one of the Earth, one of the Heavens, and a navigation instrument.

SOURCE 19
The Royal Observatory, Greenwich. This house was built by Charles II for the astronomer John Flamstead in 1675. To the right of the house is a 60-foot telescope.

RESTORATION LONDON

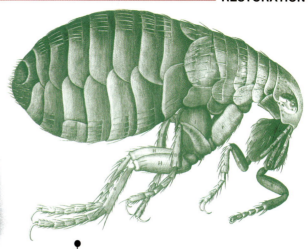

SOURCE 21
A flea seen under a microscope; a drawing from a book by Robert Hooke.

> 'To Gresham College where Mr Hooke read a very curious lecture about the recent comet proving very probably that this is the very same comet that appeared before in 1618 and that in such a time it will probably appear again, which is very new opinion . . . And this day did pay my admission money – 40s (£2) – to the Society. Here was very fine discussions and experiments; but I do lack philosophy enough to understand them, and so cannot remember them.'

SOURCE 20
Entry from Pepys's *Diary* for 1 March 1665. The Royal Society met at Gresham College. Pepys was President of the Royal Society from 1684 to 1686.

better guns and navigation instruments. Others were interested in a scientific approach to farming. The foundations of the Agrarian Revolution of the 18th century, which you will study next year, were laid at this time. The scientists invented better tools for measuring and observing, such as the microscope, telescope, air-pump, BAROMETER and thermometer.

Isaac Newton

There was more to the Scientific Revolution than this. Scientists such as Robert Hooke, Robert Boyle and Isaac Newton were trying to find explanations for everything in the universe, from comets to fleas. Newton was born in 1642 and became Professor of Mathematics at Cambridge in 1669.

The story goes that watching an apple fall to the ground one day led him to wonder why the apple fell, and did not just stay put, or move sideways. In 1686 he showed that all objects attract each other, depending on their mass and their distance apart. Thus the huge Earth pulls the tiny apple towards it by a force called gravity. This attraction happens whether the objects are apples or planets. It is thus a 'law' of science.

Newton's scientific laws explained a great deal about how the universe worked. Despite his modest comments in Source 23, most science since his time has built on his work.

SOURCE 22
Part of one of Isaac Newton's books.

> I do not know what I may appear to the world, but to myself I seem to only have been a boy playing on the seashore . . . whilst the great ocean of truth lay all undiscovered before me.

SOURCE 23
Isaac Newton describes his work towards the end of his life.

attainment target

1 List the scientific inventions and discoveries mentioned on pages 58 to 61.

2 In what ways were they all 'scientific'?

3 Use these four pages to describe the different attitudes to the world of: Sir Matthew Hale, Charles II, Robert Hooke, Isaac Newton.

4 Suggest reasons for these differences.

61

Glossary

Ancestors
People of your family who lived before you.

Anvil
A large iron block used by a blacksmith for holding and shaping objects.

Architect
A person who designs buildings.

Assassination
The murder of an important politician.

Banished
Punished by being sent out of the country you live in.

Barometer
A tool for measuring air pressure, used in weather forecasting.

Ceremony
The words and actions of a church service as set out in a prayer book.

Churchwardens
People in a parish who care for the local church's building, decoration and furniture.

Civil war
War among people of the same country.

Coffer
A chest used for storing money.

Convulsions
Violent, rapid movements of the body muscles which a person cannot control.

Cope
A large cloak worn by a priest.

Customs
Money paid to the government when goods are taken in or out of a country.

Enclosure
Dividing up open fields by putting up fences or hedges across them.

Flageolet
A musical instrument, like a recorder.

Flogged
Whipped.

Incense
A substance used in religious ceremonies which burns with a sweet smell.

Lease
An agreement between a landlord and a tenant laying out how much rent is to be paid, for how long, etc.

Massacre
The killing of a large number of defenceless people.

Merchandise
Goods for sale.

Minister
Someone who helps the monarch to rule.

Pamphlet
A short printed booklet.

Popish
An insulting term for Roman Catholic.

Protestant
Someone who protested against the Roman Catholic Church and who set up their own church.

Roman Catholic
Someone who followed the old beliefs, with the Pope as the head of the Church.

Sacked
Destroyed by an army.

Steward
Someone who looks after a house or lands for a lord or lady.

Stocks
A kind of public punishment in which the person sat with their feet held between two pieces of wood.

Tranquillity
Peace.

Tyrant
A ruler who rules badly and unfairly.

Vestments
Special clothes worn during religious ceremonies.

Index

Page numbers in **bold** refer to illustrations/captions

Acts of Union
  with Scotland, 49
  with Wales, 13
Anne, 49, **49**
anti-Catholicism, 31, 47, **51**, **52**
Aske, Robert, 13

Banqueting House, **32**
beggars, 28–29, **28**
Bible, 8, 14, 17, 50
Boleyn, Anne, 9, **9**, 10
Bosworth, battle of, 7
Boxford church, **14**, **16**, 17
Boyne, battle of the, 52, **53**
Bradshaw, John, 42, **43**
Buckingham, George
  Villiers, Duke of, 33–35, **33**
Bury St Edmunds, 12

Campion, Edmund, 17
Catherine of Aragon, 9, **9**, 10
cavaliers, 40
Charles I, **30**, **34**, 34–43, **39**, **42**
Charles II, 45, 46, **46**, 47, 58–60, **60**
Charles V, Emperor, 9
Civil War, English, 38–41
Cobham, Lord, 3, **3**
coffee houses, 54, **55**
Cranmer, Thomas, 10, 14–16
Cromwell, Oliver, 41, 42, **44**, 44–46, 52
Cromwell, Richard, 45
Cromwell, Thomas, 10, **10**, 11, 12, 13
customs duties, 36, **36**

Devon Prayer Book rebellion, 15, **15**
Diggers, 45
Dissolution of the Monasteries, 11–12, 19, 34
Divine Right of Kings, 32–34
Drake, Francis, 17

Edward VI, 14, **16**
Elizabeth I, **16**, 17, **20**
enclosures, 28–29

Fairfax, Sir Thomas, 42
farming, 24–25, 27, 28, **29**
Fawkes, Guy, 31
Field of the Cloth of Gold, 7, **7**
Flodden, battle of, 8
Foxe's Book of Martyrs, 17, **17**
France, 7, 8, 35, 36, 48, 52
Francis I, 6, 7

Galileo, 58
Glastonbury Abbey, 11
Glorious Revolution, 47, 48
Gunpowder Plot, 31, **31**

Hale, Sir Matthew, 58
Hampden, John, 36, **36**
Hanover, 49
Hardwick, Bess of, 26, **26**
Hardwick Hall, 26, **26**
Harvey, William, 59
Hearne, Thomas, 25
Henry VII, 7, 13
Henry VIII, 6–10, 13, 14, **16**
Hooke, Robert, 60, **61**
Hopkins, Matthew, 58
houses, 18, 19, 22–26
Hyde, Edward, Earl of Clarendon, 39, 40

inns, 22, **22**
inventories, **23**, 25
Ireland, 38, 50–53

James I, 30, **30**, 31–34
James II, **46**, 47, 52
jousting, 6
Justices of the Peace (JPs), 13, 21

Laud, William, 37, **37**, 38
Lee, Rowland, 13
Levellers, 45
London
  Great Fire of, 56–57, **56**
  Great Plague of, 55, **55**
  life in, 22, 54–57
Luther, Martin, 8

Marritt, William, 22, 23, **23**
Marston Moor, battle of, 41
Marvell, Andrew, 43
Mary I, 9, 16, **16**
Mary II, 47–49
Mary Rose, **8**
medicine, 27, 59, **59**
merchants, 22–23
monasteries, 11, **11**, 12
money, 20, 25
monks, 11, 12
Montacute House, 18–19, **19**
More, Sir Thomas, 6, 10, **10**
Morgan, William, 17
Muchelney Abbey, 11, **11**, 12

Navy, 8, 40, 54
New Model Army, 41–42, 44–45
new monarchy, 6, 7
Newton, Isaac, 61

Orrery, Earl of, 58, **58**

Parliament, 10, 13, 33, 35–41, **38**, 45–49, **49**
Pepys, Samuel, 54–57, **54**, 60–61
Pilgrim Fathers, 33
Pilgrimage of Grace, 13, **13**
plantations, 50–51, **51**
Poor Law 1601, 29
poor people, 25–29
puritans, 17, 33, **35**, 37, **37**, 41, 46
Pym, John, **35**, 35, 37–39, 40

Quakers, 46, 48, **48**

religion
  Catholicism, 9, 12, **12**, 16, 17, 31, 35, 47, 48, 52–53
  Protestantism, 8, 14, 15, **15**, 16, 17, 37, 52–53
Richard III, 7
roundheads, 40
royal finances, 11, 34–36, 48
Royal Society, 58, **60**, 61
Rupert, Prince, 40

science, 58–61
scientific instruments, **58**, **59**, 60
Scotland, 8, 31, 33, 37, 41, 49
ship money, 36, 38
Solway Moss, battle of, 8
Spain, 17, 28, 36, 50
Spenser, Edmund, 50, **50**
Strafford, Earl of, 38, **38**

theatres, 56
Tichborne, Sir Henry, 21, **21**
timeline, 5
towns, 22, 25, 54–57
trade, 22, 49, 56

Valor Ecclesiasticus, 11, **11**
Verney, Sir Edmund, 39, 41
Verney, Sir Ralph, 39

Wales, 13, 17, 21, 24
Welsh surnames, 13
William III, 47, **47**, 48, 49, 52–53, **53**
witches, 58, **58**
Wolsey, Cardinal Thomas, 8, 9
women, 26–27
Wyclif, John, 16

yeoman, 24

© HarperCollins*Publishers*

Christopher Culpin asserts the moral right to be identified as the author of this work.

All rights reserved. No part of this publication may be reproduced, stored in a retrieval system, or transmitted in any form or by any means, electronic, mechanical, photo-copying or otherwise, without the prior permission of the publisher.

First published 1992 by Collins Educational
An imprint of HarperCollins*Publishers*
77-85 Fulham Palace Road
London
W6 8JB

Reprinted 1992, 1996

ISBN 0 00 327243 5

Cover designed by Glynis Edwards
Book designed by Derek Lee
Series planning by Nicole Lagneau
Edited by Lorimer Poultney
Picture research by Donna Thynne
Artwork by Linda Rogers Associates/Peter Dennis (on pages 13, 14, 15, 23, 24, 37, 40, 44, 45, 49, 50, 51) and Angela
Lumley (on pages 6, 18, 30, 42, 54)
Production by Mandy Inness

Typeset by Dorchester Typesetting Group Ltd

Printed and bound in Hong Kong

Acknowledgements

Every effort has been made to contact holders of copyright material, but if any have been inadvertently overlooked the publishers will be pleased to make the necessary arrangements at the first opportunity.

Photographs The publishers would like to thank the following for permission to reproduce photographs on these pages:

T = top, C = centre, B = bottom, R = right, L = left

Ancient Art and Architecture Collection, 15; Ashmolean Museum, Oxford, 43; B. T. Batsford, 28C; Bodleian Library, Oxford, 61T, 61C; Bridgeman Art Library, 9L, 10T, 21, 33R, 46T, 55T, 56; British Library, 51B; Collections, 31B; Courtauld institute, London, 57B; English Heritage, 13L; e. t. archive, 60T; Frick Collection, New York, 10B; By gracious permission of Her Majesty the Queen, 7, 34, 35T, 47, 49; Michael Holford, 55B; Hulton Picture Company, 25C, 27, 29T, 29C, 30B, 35B; Impact/Pamla Toler, 24; Michael Jenner, 22; A. F. Kersting, 32R; Lambeth Palace Library, London, 58T; Pepys Library, Magdalene College, Cambridge, 8, 57T; Mansell Collection, 12, 17, 41, 44R; By courtesy of the Director, National Army Museum, London, 53T; National Galleries of Scotland, 30C, 42; National Maritime Museum, 60B; National Museum of Wales/Sudeley Castle, 16; National Portrait Gallery, London, 9R, 31T, 33, 44B, 46B, 54; The National Trust, 18, 19R, 26T, 26B; Pacemaker, 53B; Private collection, 20; Public Record Office, London, 11R; Rex Features, 44L, 44C; Steve Richards, 28T; Royal Armouries, 6, 40; Somerset County Council Environment Department, 19L; Sotherby's, 58B; South Somerset District Council, 48; Syndication International, 36; Victoria and Albert Museum, London 25T; Weidenfeld Archive, 38; Wellcome Institute Library, London, 59.

Cover photograph: e. t. archive.